Government Procedures and Operations

Government Procedures and Operations

COVID-19 in Nursing Homes: Impact, Transmission and Prevention
Fred C. Wallace (Editor)
2023. ISBN: 979-8-88697-673-1 (Hardcover)
2023. ISBN: 979-8-88697-683-0 (eBook)

The Significance of the COVID Pandemic in Nursing Homes
John S. Gill (Editor)
2023. ISBN: 979-8-88697-660-1 (Hardcover)
2023. ISBN: 979-8-88697-682-3 (eBook)

Putting an End to Surprise Medical Billing
Danial E. Tackett (Editor)
2022. ISBN: 979-8-88697-296-2 (Hardcover)
2022. ISBN: 979-8-88697-327-3 (eBook)

Abortion Rights, Access, and Legislative Response
Jorge P. Sandford (Editor)
2022. ISBN: 979-8-88697-258-0 (Softcover)
2022. ISBN: 979-8-88697-294-8 (eBook)

Review of Capitol Police Procedures During the Capitol Attack
Rafael B. Phillips (Editor)
2022. ISBN: 979-8-88697-260-3 (Hardcover)
2022. ISBN: 978-1-53617-478-6 (eBook)

More information about this series can be found at
https://novapublishers.com/product-category/series/government-procedures-and-operations/

Michael V. Walls
Editor

Infrastructure Cybersecurity

Protections, Threats, and Federal Programs

Copyright © 2023 by Nova Science Publishers, Inc.

All rights reserved. No part of this book may be reproduced, stored in a retrieval system or transmitted in any form or by any means: electronic, electrostatic, magnetic, tape, mechanical photocopying, recording or otherwise without the written permission of the Publisher.

We have partnered with Copyright Clearance Center to make it easy for you to obtain permissions to reuse content from this publication. Please visit copyright.com and search by Title, ISBN, or ISSN.

For further questions about using the service on copyright.com, please contact:

	Copyright Clearance Center	
Phone: +1-(978) 750-8400	Fax: +1-(978) 750-4470	E-mail: info@copyright.com

NOTICE TO THE READER

The Publisher has taken reasonable care in the preparation of this book but makes no expressed or implied warranty of any kind and assumes no responsibility for any errors or omissions. No liability is assumed for incidental or consequential damages in connection with or arising out of information contained in this book. The Publisher shall not be liable for any special, consequential, or exemplary damages resulting, in whole or in part, from the readers' use of, or reliance upon, this material. Any parts of this book based on government reports are so indicated and copyright is claimed for those parts to the extent applicable to compilations of such works.

Independent verification should be sought for any data, advice or recommendations contained in this book. In addition, no responsibility is assumed by the Publisher for any injury and/or damage to persons or property arising from any methods, products, instructions, ideas or otherwise contained in this publication.

This publication is designed to provide accurate and authoritative information with regards to the subject matter covered herein. It is sold with the clear understanding that the Publisher is not engaged in rendering legal or any other professional services. If legal or any other expert assistance is required, the services of a competent person should be sought. FROM A DECLARATION OF PARTICIPANTS JOINTLY ADOPTED BY A COMMITTEE OF THE AMERICAN BAR ASSOCIATION AND A COMMITTEE OF PUBLISHERS.

Library of Congress Cataloging-in-Publication Data

ISBN: 979-8-89113-039-5

Published by Nova Science Publishers, Inc. † New York

Contents

Preface		vii
Chapter 1	**Threats to Critical Infrastructure: Examining the Colonial Pipeline Cyberattack**	1
	Committee on Homeland Security and Governmental Affairs	
Chapter 2	**Pipeline Cybersecurity: Federal Programs**	55
	Paul W. Parfomak and Chris Jaikaran	
Chapter 3	**Transportation Cybersecurity: Protecting Planes, Trains, and Pipelines from Cyber Threats**	85
	Committee on Homeland Security	
Index		163

Preface

Private entities, especially those critical to our nation's infrastructure, are responsible for assessing their individual risk and investing in technology to prevent breaches. At the same time, the federal government must develop a comprehensive approach to not only defend against cyberattacks, but also to punish foreign adversaries who continue to perpetrate them. This book examines policies that will help secure our critical infrastructure networks.

Chapter 1

Threats to Critical Infrastructure: Examining the Colonial Pipeline Cyberattack*

Committee on Homeland Security and Governmental Affairs

Tuesday, June 8, 2021
U.S. Senate
Washington, DC.

The Committee met, pursuant to notice, at 10:04 a.m., via Webex and in room SD–342, Dirksen Senate Office Building, Hon. Gary C. Peters, Chairman of the Committee, presiding.

Present: Senators Peters, Carper, Hassan, Sinema, Rosen, Padilla, Ossoff, Portman, Johnson, Lankford, Romney, Scott, and Hawley.

Opening Statement of Chairman Peters[1]

Chairman PETERS. The Committee will come to order.

Mr. Blount, welcome to the Committee, and thank you for joining us for this important discussion on the harmful cyberattack against your company, Colonial Pipeline, and how we can work together to strengthen our coordination and response to this very serious cybersecurity incident.

---

* This is an edited, reformatted and augmented version of the Hearing Before the Committee on Homeland Security and Governmental Affairs, United States Senate, Publication No. S. Hrg. 117–429, dated June 8, 2021.
[1] The prepared statement of Senator Peters appears in the Appendix.

In: Infrastructure Cybersecurity
Editor: Michael V. Walls
ISBN: 979-8-89113-039-5
© 2023 Nova Science Publishers, Inc.

When Colonial Pipeline was forced to shut down operations last month due to a ransomware attack, millions of Americans up and down the East Coast had their lives disrupted by gas shortages and price increases. In the weeks since your company was struck, we have seen a series of other attacks on everything from our transportation networks to meatpacking centers.

Just today we learned of additional intrusions into Internet platforms. Those private sector strikes follow especially damaging attacks on our Federal Government, including the extensive SolarWinds hack earlier this year.

While the objectives of these attacks differ, they all demonstrate that bad actors, whether criminal organizations or foreign governments, are always looking to exploit the weakest link, infiltrate networks, steal information, and disrupt American life.

Mr. Blount, I am glad your company continues to recover from this malicious attack and that the Federal Bureau of Investigation (FBI) was able to recover millions of dollars in ransom paid. But I am alarmed that this breach ever occurred in the first place and that communities from Texas to New York suffered as a result.

I appreciate that you have joined us today to provide answers to the Committee and the American people on how a group of criminals was able to infiltrate your networks, steal nearly 100 gigabytes (GB) of data in two hours, and then lock your systems with ransomware to demand payment. I am also looking forward to hearing an update on your progress to recover from this serious breach.

Private entities, especially those that are critical to our Nation's infrastructure, are responsible for assessing their individual risk and investing in the technology to prevent breaches and to ensure that they can continue to provide service to customers who rely on them for basic necessities like fuel.

At the same time, the Federal Government must develop a comprehensive, all-of-government approach to not only defend against cyberattacks, but punish foreign adversaries who continue to perpetrate them or harbor criminal organizations that target American systems.

This approach requires bolstering our defenses and using the full might of our diplomatic, military, and intelligence capabilities.

We must also ensure private entities like Colonial are providing the Federal Government with timely and relevant information in the event of a major incident. We need Federal agencies charged with cybersecurity like the Department of Homeland Security (DHS) and the Cybersecurity and Infrastructure Security Agency (CISA) to understand the extent of these attacks and how best to support victims.

Make no mistake. If we do not step up our cybersecurity readiness, the consequences will be severe. The ransomware attack on Colonial Pipeline affected millions of Americans. The next time an incident like this happens, unfortunately, it could be even worse. As Chairman of this Committee, I am committed to prioritizing policies that will help secure our critical infrastructure networks, including in the proposed infrastructure package Congress is now negotiating.

Protecting the American people from these sophisticated, harmful, and growing attacks will not be easy. We must learn from our past mistakes, find out what went wrong, and work together to tackle this enormous challenge. Inaction, however, is simply not an option.

With that, I will turn it over to Ranking Member Portman for your opening remarks.

Opening Statement of Senator Portman[2]

Senator PORTMAN. Thank you, Mr. Chairman. Mr. Blount, thank you for being here today. We are going to get into some tough questioning, and, unfortunately, what happened to your company is not an isolated incident.

We have had some good bipartisan work over the years to improve cybersecurity on this Committee with you, Senator Peters, with you, Senator Johnson, and others. Let us face it, there is a lot more to do. What happened with regard to Colonial Pipeline is one example. This is about ransomware attacks on critical infra structure, and that is the topic of the hearing broadly today. This paralyzes a company by locking its computer systems, holding its data and operations hostage until ransom paid.

Interestingly, these ransoms are not on the company itself, typically. Increasingly, the hackers also pursue a two-pronged ransom approach where they download and threaten to release sensitive victim data so individuals, say your customers, may also have been subject to ransomware.

There seems to be a new ransomware attack every week. We are going to hear today again about Colonial Pipeline and some of the details there, but no entity, public or private, is safe from these attacks. Last week, we learned that ransomware shut down the world's largest meat processor, JBS, including nine beef plants in the United States. Both the Colonial Pipeline attack and JBS attacks were attributed to a Russian criminal organization, by the way.

---

[2] The prepared statement of Senator Portman appears in the Appendix.

Just this morning, news broke that a constituent outreach services platform that nearly 60 offices in the U.S. Congress, the House of Representatives, uses was hit with a ransomware attack. As I have said before, no one is safe from these attacks, including us. I hope that we will cover four specific areas here today. One is we have to understand that these attacks have real-world consequences. On May 7th, Colonial Pipeline learned they suffered a ransomware attack impacting their information technology (IT), systems by this Russian-based criminal group called "DarkSide." Recent news reports indicate that hackers accessed the Colonial system through a compromised password of a virtual private network (VPN) account. This account did not use multifactor authentication (MAF), which is a very basic cybersecurity best practice. We will talk more about that and why they did not. This easily allowed the hackers to gain access.

Colonial moved quickly to disconnect their operational system to prevent hackers from moving laterally and accessing those systems. That, of course, although an appropriate response to a cyberattack made Colonial's critical pipelines unusable, and that was a huge problem. So real-world consequences, 45 percent of the East Coast fuel was coming from Colonial. With operations shut down, people across the East Coast bought fuel in a panic, unsure how long the shortage would last. A lot of service stations ran out of fuel altogether, so people could not get gas, could not get to work. Of course, prices skyrocketed. Again, real-world consequences.

Second, I hope today we will talk about how this shows the difficult decision ransomware victims face. Should they pay the ransom or not? The U.S. Government has a position on this. Both CISA at the Department of Homeland Security and the FBI strongly recommend organizations do not pay ransoms. Why? Because paying ransoms rewards ransomware hackers. If no one paid ransoms, criminals would have little incentive to engage in ransomware attacks. Even if an entity pays, there is no guarantee that the hackers will give them the decryption key or not strike again, and we will talk more about that, too, in terms of this incident.

However, organizations obviously have to weigh these consequences against keeping the operations offline, in this case limiting 45 percent of the East Coast fuel supply. Colonial Pipeline paid DarkSide a ransom, we are told, of 75 bitcoins worth over $4 million at the time. Yesterday the good news is the Department of Justice (DOJ) announced the recovery of 63.7 of those bitcoins, but DOJ will not be able to recover those ransom payments in other cases. We will talk more about that and how they did it and what that means.

I appreciate Mr. Blount's transparency in acknowledging that his company paid the $4.4 million in ransom. I hope today we can explore the reasons for that decision.

    Third, this attack demonstrates the gaps in information sharing between these impacted organizations and the Federal Government. Last month, Brandon Wales was before us in that very seat. He is the Acting Director of CISA. He testified in response to one of my questions that he did not think Colonial Pipeline would have contacted CISA at all if the FBI did not bring it to them. CISA's authorities allow the agency to engage on a voluntary basis when requested by an affected organization, and CISA has the Federal Government's best practices as to how to deal with these cyberattacks, and it was set up at the Department of Homeland Security for that purpose.

    While I think that CISA being able to engage is the right approach, they must have relevant information to be able to share it among other critical infrastructure owners and operators who may be similarly targeted. We have to get them that information, and there is a gap now.

    Finally, we have to recognize these ransomware attacks for what they are. It is a serious national security threat. Attacks against critical infrastructure are not just attacks on companies. They are attacks on our country itself. When DarkSide attacked Colonial Pipeline, it was not a company that was affected. Americans across the East Coast felt the squeeze at fuel pumps when Colonial shut off nearly 50 percent of the fuel supply.

    The criminals conducting these attacks often operate with at least the tacit acceptance and approval of the foreign governments they operate out of. The U.S. Government needs to take stronger steps to hold these countries like Russia accountable. At the upcoming summit with President Putin and President Biden, one would hope that this is going to be at the top of the agenda.

    Ransomware attacks will continue to plague U.S. companies and critical infrastructure. As the Committee of jurisdiction over both cybersecurity and critical infrastructure security, we need to reevaluate how we defend against ransomware and identify solutions to mitigate the consequences of these attacks.

    Thank you, Mr. Chairman.
    Chairman PETERS. Thank you, Senator Portman.
    Mr. Blount, it is the practice of the Homeland Security and Governmental Affairs Committee (HSGAC) to swear in witnesses, so if you will stand and raise your right hand, please. Do you swear that the testimony you will give

before this Committee will be the truth, the whole truth, and nothing but the truth, so help you, God?

Mr. BLOUNT. I do.

Chairman PETERS. Thank you. You may be seated.

Mr. Joseph Blount is the president and Chief Executive Officer (CEO) of Colonial Pipeline. He joined Colonial in October 2017 with more than three decades of experience in the energy industry. Mr. Blount previously served as CEO of Century Midstream LLC, a company which he co-founded. Mr. Blount has also spent 10 years with Unocal Corporation and ultimately served as president and chief operating officer (COO) of Unocal Midstream and Trade.

Mr. Blount, welcome to the Committee. We look forward to your testimony and appreciate your willingness to answer our questions. You are recognized for your seven-minute opening statement.

Testimony of Joseph Blount,[3] President and Chief Executive Officer, Colonial Pipeline

Mr. BLOUNT. Chairman Peters, Ranking Member Portman, and Members of the Committee, my name is Joe Blount, and since 2017 I have served as the president and CEO of Colonial Pipeline Company. Thank you for the opportunity to testify before the Committee today.

Since 1962, we have been shipping and transporting refined products to the market. Our pipeline system spans over 5,500 miles and is one of the most complex pieces of energy infrastructure in America, if not the world. On any given day, we transport more than 100 million gallons of gasoline, diesel, jet fuel, and other refined products. Shipping that product safely and securely is what we do.

The product we transport accounts for nearly half the fuel consumed on the East Coast, providing energy for more than 50 million Americans. Americans rely on us to get fuel to the pump, but so do cities and local governments. We supply fuel for critical operations, such as airports, ambulances, and first responders.

The safety and security of our pipeline system is something we take very seriously, and we always operate with the interests of our customers, shippers, and country first in mind.

---

[3] The prepared statement of Mr. Blount appears in the Appendix.

Just 1 month ago, we were the victims of a ransomware attack by a cyber criminal group, and that attack encrypted our IT systems. Although the investigation is still ongoing, we believe the attacker exploited the legacy VPN profile that was not intended to be in use.

DarkSide demanded a financial payment in exchange for a key to unlock the impacted systems. We had cyber defenses in place, but the unfortunate reality is that those defenses were compromised.

The attack forced us to make difficult choices in real time that no company ever wants to face, but I am proud of the way our people reacted quickly to isolate and contain the attack so that we could get the pipeline back up and running safely. I am also very grateful for the immediate and sustained support of law enforcement and Federal authorities, including the White House. We reached out to Federal authorities within hours of the attack, and they have continued to be true allies as we have worked to quickly and safely restore our operations. I especially want to thank the Department of Justice and the FBI for their leadership and the progress they announced earlier this week.

I also want to express my gratitude to the employees at Colonial Pipeline and the American people for your actions and support as we responded to the attack and dealt with the disruption that it caused. We are deeply sorry for the impact that this attack had, but we are also heartened by the resilience of our country and of our company.

Finally, I want to address two additional issues that I know are on your minds, and I am going to address them the only way I know how: directly and honestly.

First, the ransom payment. I made the decision to pay, and I made the decision to keep the information about the payment as confidential as possible. It was the hardest decision I have made in my 39 years in the energy industry, and I know how critical our pipeline is to the country, and I put the interests of the country first.

I kept the information closely held because we were concerned about operational safety and security, and we wanted to stay focused on getting the pipeline back up and running. I believe with all my heart it was the right choice to make, but I want to respect those who see this issue differently.

I also now state publicly that we quietly and quickly worked with law enforcement in this matter from the start, which may have helped lead to the substantial recovery of funds announced by the DOJ this week.

Second, we are further hardening our cyber defenses. We have rebuilt and restored our critical IT systems and are continuing to enhance our safeguards.

But we are not where I want us to be. If our chief information officer (CIO) needs resources, she will get them.

We have also brought in several of the world's leading experts to help us fully understand what happened and how we can continue, in partnership with you, to add defenses and resiliency to our networks. I especially want to thank Mandiant, Dragos, and Black Hills on the consultant side, in the White House, and all the government agencies who assisted us both with the criminal investigation and with the restart of the pipeline. We are already working to implement the recent guidance and directives on cybersecurity. Our forensic work continues, and we will learn more in the months ahead. I appreciate your support and look forward to our discussion today.

Chairman PETERS. Thank you, Mr. Blount

Mr. Blount, Colonial is one of hundreds of victims of ransomware attacks against our Nation's critical infrastructure this year. Would you think and would you agree with the statement that the Federal Government should be doing more to help companies like yours prevent cyberattacks?

Mr. BLOUNT. Thank you for that question, Mr. Chairman. First, I would like to state that as a private entity we know we have a responsibility as well. We are accountable for our defenses and our reaction to attacks like this. But I think if we look at the number of incidents that are taking place today throughout the world, let alone here in America, private industry alone cannot do everything, cannot solve the problem totally by themselves. The partnership between private and government is very important to fight this ongoing onslaught of cyberattacks around the world.

Chairman PETERS. CISA is the main Federal domestic cybersecurity agency, and it hosts the Pipeline Sector Coordinating Council (SCC) to help bring together the private sector and government in that partnership, as you mentioned, to identify and address security issues. Do you know if Colonial ever participated in these meetings or any other exercise or events that were hosted by CISA?

Mr. BLOUNT. Thank you for that question, Mr. Chairman. I know that CISA is a good organization, and I know that we maintain a lot of communication and contact with CISA and have historically between our CIO and representatives from CISA. Actually, I was somewhat disappointed when I heard that they felt like if we had not gone in and contacted them the first day with the FBI that we would not have contacted them separately. If you go back and look at the record and look at who we contacted throughout the event, we talked to every entity that could possibly help us get through the condition that we found ourselves in that day.

Chairman PETERS. Do you know if you participated in any of those meetings?

Mr. BLOUNT. Yes, Senator, we participate in every governmental opportunity that we have to do tabletop exercise, security screens, and things like that.

Chairman PETERS. You mentioned that you did not contact CISA directly. Why did Colonial Pipeline decide to forgo contacting or notifying CISA directly? What was the rationale for that?

Mr. BLOUNT. Thank you, Mr. Chairman. We contacted the FBI almost immediately that morning once we determined that we were under attack. In that conversation with the FBI that morning, they frankly said, "We want to get on a phone call later today. We are going to bring CISA into the conversation." At that point we already knew the contact would be made there. We had a lot of governmental entities to respond to that day and call directly, and that was the most efficient means. We knew they would be in that meeting, and they were indeed in that meeting right after noon the day of the 7th.

Chairman PETERS. As you mentioned in your opening comments and you have reiterated here in answers to these questions, you have been working closely with the FBI, and I know you allowed Mandiant, the private security firm, which you also referenced in your opening, to share information with CISA, and that is happening now.

Given those actions, I would suspect that you agree that you have a responsibility to protect other potential victims based on what you have learned. To what extent do you believe that responsibility extends?

Mr. BLOUNT. Thank you for that question, Mr. Chairman. We have been very transparent from the start. If you looked at who we contacted that day, we started with the FBI. Obviously, they included in the follow-up conversation. Then we started marching through all the ones that we normally would report to, whether it is the Federal Energy Regulatory Commission (FERC), Pipeline and Hazardous Materials Safety Administration (PHMSA), Department of Energy (DOE), et cetera, et cetera. What we found during that day was that we were allowed the conduit through DOE to talk to all these organizations on an ongoing basis, but through one central briefing.

We found that the ability to have that conduit, to work on the supply side of the equation, and on the restoration side of the equation, with any number of governmental entities was extremely helpful to us. Then, of course, on the investigative side, we had the FBI and CISA working on that.

For anybody that comes under an attack like this, what you cannot re-create is time and space and the ability to respond. The ability to have the conduit both on the investigative side as well as on the restoration and on the supply side was extremely helpful to Colonial Pipeline and our employees. It was an all-hands-on-deck situation that morning and throughout the event.

Chairman PETERS. Prior to the attack, I know you are not a technical expert, but it would have been helpful for you to get information about other potential attacks or other companies that may have been attacked with similar types of cyber incidents?

Mr. BLOUNT. Yes, Mr. Chairman. For example, we gave a lot of indications of compromise to the FBI and CISA during the days of the event, and I think what we saw as an industry is immediately that material was dispersed out, and in the case of the internet protocol (IP) addresses, I believe CISA actually posted those. And that was a means for us once again to efficiently communicate to our industry partners what was going on. In addition to that, go back to the first day when we were contacting people, we made initial contact with some of our industry trade groups to tell them what we could possibly tell them at that point in time. So we have been, once again, very open and transparent, hoping that everybody could not only be aware of the situation, but think about what they could do to help prevent that from occurring in their own company.

Chairman PETERS. That is all very encouraging to hear, and for the record, I am working on legislation right now to make sure that information is indeed being shared with CISA to get a better understanding of what is happening in ransomware, not just with your company but across the board.

Reporting indicates and you have affirmed today that you made the decision to pay the ransom of $4.4 million. We are certainly happy to see that a portion of that is being recovered by the Department of Justice now. My question to you, though, is: Prior to making the decision to pay the ransom, had you consulted with anyone in the Federal Government on whether that would be an appropriate response?

Mr. BLOUNT. Thank you for that question, Mr. Chairman. It was our understanding that the decision was solely ours as a private company to make the decision about whether to pay or not to pay. Considering the consequences of potentially not bringing the pipeline back on as quickly as I possibly could, I chose the option to make the ransom payment in order to get all the tools necessary and the optionality of those tools to bring the pipeline on as quick as we possibly could, safely as well as securely.

Chairman PETERS. After you paid the ransom and received the key to unlock your systems, did that actually fix all of the problems? Where are you today? How long do you think it will take for you to be 100 percent?

Mr. BLOUNT. That is a great question, Mr. Chairman. Thank you for asking it. I think what a lot of people do not realize about cyberattacks and the repercussions of a cyberattack is it takes months and months and months, and in some cases, what we have heard from other companies that have been impacted, years to restore your systems. Our focus that first week was to restore the critical systems that we needed on the IT side in order to safely and securely bring our pipeline system back up. So that is what we focused on.

An example would be this week we are bringing back online seven finance systems that we have not had since the morning of May 7th. Again, the remediation is ongoing, and, again, that is why you bring someone like a Mandiant in immediately, one, to help investigate the situation, but also to help restore what you have lost throughout the process.

The keys are helpful, and we have used the keys, so they have been advantageous to us. But they are not perfect.

Chairman PETERS. I think that is important to remember. You get the keys, but you still have a problem for many months and a lot of work to do.

Mr. BLOUNT. Yes, sir, that is correct.

Chairman PETERS. It really illustrates the seriousness of what we are dealing with. Thank you for your answers.

Ranking Member Portman, you are recognized for your questions.

Senator PORTMAN. Thank you, Mr. Chairman.

Mr. Blount, you are a victim, and we understand that. And yet we are trying to provide oversight and even provide some new laws potentially to try to deal with this increasing and really dramatic issue of cyberattacks, and specifically today talking about ransomware. Let us clarify the record. You made your ransomware payment to the hackers on the day you discovered it. Is that correct?

Mr. BLOUNT. Ranking Member, thank you for that question. We did not. We made the decision that evening to negotiate with——

Senator PORTMAN. So that was the evening of May 7th?

Mr. BLOUNT. Yes, sir.

Senator PORTMAN. And so you did not make the payment until when?

Mr. BLOUNT. The payment was made the following day.

Senator PORTMAN. May 8th.

Mr. BLOUNT. Yes, sir.

Senator PORTMAN. And you indicated today that the FBI was in discussions with you on May 7th. Is that correct?

Mr. BLOUNT. Ranking Member Portman, that is correct. Yes, sir.
Senator PORTMAN. What did the FBI tell you? What did they advise you to do with regard to paying the ransom?

Mr. BLOUNT. Ranking Member Portman, I was not involved in those conversations with the FBI, but in discussions with my team, I do not believe the discussion about the ransom actually took place the first day, on May 7th. The focus more was on getting to the proper centers of expertise with the FBI. In this case, I believe it was the San Francisco office. We started with the Atlanta office in our notification. And then it was a function of starting—they already started to collect data from us, indications of compromise and——

Senator PORTMAN. So their official position is you should not pay ransoms, and yet they did not communicate that to you as far as you know?

Mr. BLOUNT. Ranking Member Portman, of course, I was not in that conversation. I cannot confirm or deny that. But I do agree that their position is they do not encourage the payment of ransom. It is a company decision to make.

Senator PORTMAN. Yes, and so you knew what their advice was going to be even if they did not provide it that day?

Mr. BLOUNT. Ranking Member Portman, yes, sir, we did.

Senator PORTMAN. OK. Did you talk to the Treasury Department's Office of Foreign Assets Control (OFAC)? This is the office that is charged with sanctions, and so if you are a sanctioned individual and you make a payment, as you know, there are potential violations of law. Did you contact Treasury Department's Office of Foreign Assets Control?

Mr. BLOUNT. Ranking Member Portman, the day that we decided to negotiate, we hired experts both on the legal side as well as on the negotiation side. We did not have any direct contact with DarkSide ourselves. I can assure you that everyone involved in that process continually went and fact-checked to make sure that this was not an OFAC-listed entity.

Senator PORTMAN. So you were in touch with OFAC to ensure you were not paying the ransom to a sanctioned entity or to a sanctioned individual?

Mr. BLOUNT. Ranking Member Portman, I was not involved in those conversations, and so I cannot attest to who actually talked to who. But I do know that repeatedly throughout the process the fact of whether DarkSide was on the sanctions list or not was factchecked repeatedly.

Senator PORTMAN. OK. We may have some follow-up questions on that just to figure out what the relationship was there. Again, this is about looking forward, how do we avoid this situation where sanctioned individuals or entities are getting a ransom payment, which would be a violation of Federal law.

The Wall Street Journal says that the decryption tool did not really work, so you paid the ransom, they give you the decryption tool to be able to undo the harm that they did. That is how it normally works. And yet the decryption tool was not effective. Is that correct?

Mr. BLOUNT. Ranking Member Portman, the encryption tool is an option that is made available to you, and when you are looking at bringing critical structure back up as quickly as you possibly can, you want to make every option available to you that you can. Mandiant can be the best one to answer about how important the encryption tool was restoring the critical options we needed within the first couple days.

Senator PORTMAN. Did the decryption tool work?

Mr. BLOUNT. It has worked, yes, sir.

Senator PORTMAN. The Wall Street Journal story was inaccurate, it was effective?

Mr. BLOUNT. Ranking Member Portman, I think that article came out pretty early on, so I would say that we know subsequently that the de-encryption tool actually does work to some degree. As I stated earlier, it is not a perfect tool.

Senator PORTMAN. OK. It was provided to you by the hackers, correct?

Mr. BLOUNT. Ranking Member Portman, yes, sir, that is correct.

Senator PORTMAN. OK. There are also news reports about how this happened. As I said in my opening statement, there was a compromised password of a virtual private network account. This account apparently did not use multifactor authentication, which, again, is kind of a basic cybersecurity hygiene item that, companies should have in place, making it harder for people to gain access.

Prior to the attack, did your company require all employees to use multifactor authentication?

Mr. BLOUNT. Ranking Member Portman, in the case of this particular legacy VPN, it did only have single-factor authentication. It was a complicated password, so I want to be clear on that. It was not a "Colonial 123" type password. The investigation is ongoing by Mandiant to try to determine how that material was compromised. But in our normal operation, we use an RSA token allowance in order to create authentication difficulties for remote access.

Senator PORTMAN. Would your advice going forward be that multifactor authentication ought to be used?

Mr. BLOUNT. Ranking Member Portman, that is absolutely the correct advice.

Senator PORTMAN. The Transportation Security Administration (TSA) has given the industry a lot of leeway. Critical infrastructure and voluntary compliance has been the approach. They came out late last month, after your attack, with some new directives, and now there is a mandate that reporting cyberattacks must happen; they must go to CISA, which is, again, this group within the Department of Homeland Security, and then it will be shared with TSA. You have a designated cybersecurity coordinator within the company, and you have to review your current activities against their recommendations on cyber risks, identify gaps, and develop remediation measures. Do you support that?

Mr. BLOUNT. Ranking Member Portman, if you look at our actions starting on May 7th, we almost to the "T" duplicated what the new standards are, and we are in full compliance today as well.

Senator PORTMAN. I had mentioned earlier that, we have written legislation in this Committee over the years to try to deal with cybersecurity. Pretty much every member here today has been involved with that. As I said earlier, we obviously need to do more. The question is: With regard to critical infrastructure in particular, should there be more mandates? And now there is, and they have the authority to do this under a 2007 law, it appears. Now there is this mandate on reporting it, a mandate on having a coordinator. But, still, there is not a mandate saying that you have to do certain things in terms of best practices or good cyber hygiene. Do you think there should be additional requirements from TSA with regard to critical infrastructure?

Mr. BLOUNT. Ranking Member Portman, first I would like to thank you for your leadership on these issues in the past, but certainly on a go-forward basis, I think anything that can help industry have better security practices, standards to follow, would be extremely helpful, especially for the smaller companies that are in other industries as well as my industry, less sophisticated.

Senator PORTMAN. Thank you, Mr. Chairman.

Chairman PETERS. Thank you, Senator Portman.

Senator CARPER, you are recognized for your questions.

Opening Statement of Senator Carper

Senator CARPER. Thanks, Mr. Chairman.

Mr. Blount, thank you very much for joining us. The fact that you and your employees, your company, and those who have been certainly consumers that have been harmed by this, but we regret that. But if you had the opportunity to speak to other people, your counterparts in businesses around the country, maybe give them two or three words of advice to help them with this sort of thing, what would you say?

Mr. BLOUNT. Senator, that is a great question, and if I could boil it down to two or three words of advice, as you suggested, I would suggest that we certainly take a look at our defenses, and even though we felt comfortably historically that we are where we felt we needed to be to protect our assets, this threat grows every day. The sophistication of this threat grows every day. So let us make sure that we are keeping our eye on that.

And then the other side of the equation is if you wind up in a situation like we found ourselves on May 7th, have an emergency response process that allows you to respond quickly and, most importantly, to be extremely transparent and to contact the authorities who indeed do have resources that potentially could help you through a very difficult process.

Senator CARPER. Thank you. Abraham Lincoln was once asked, "What is the role of government?" And he responded, "The role of government is to do for the people what they cannot do for themselves." With respect to one of the things—I have been on this Committee for about 20 years, and we have spent a lot of time trying to figure out what is the role of government, especially with respect to cybersecurity, but my question is: What do you believe the appropriate role for government is, should be, should have been? How do we measure up? What did we do well or what could we have done better?

Mr. BLOUNT. Senator, thank you for that question. Obviously, with the threat that we have in this country and around the world today, I think the private-public partnership is extremely important. We can do things as private industry to protect our facilities and assets and be safe cybersecurity-wise. But there are things around the world that we obviously have no ability to participate, and that is pressure on foreign governments that harbor criminals and people like this, and that is where government comes into play. As a company that has been regulated for over 57 years, regulation is not foreign to us, and we think regulation can be healthy. And so we support anything that helps further protect these critical assets that we all rely upon for our daily life.

Senator CARPER. As I am sure you know, there are numerous government agencies that are involved in trying to secure critical infrastructure, all kinds of infrastructure, specifically pipelines. The Transportation Security Administration is in charge of Federal programs for pipeline security, but most people think of TSA as they are going to the airport, going through airport security, but they do a lot of other things, for the most part doing them, I think, very well. But the TSA works closely with the Department of Transportation's Pipeline and Hazardous Materials Safety Administration as well as folks at the Department of Energy and the Federal Energy Regulatory Commission. That is just a handful of government agencies that are working to secure our Nation's pipelines, and that type of coordination among agencies requires continued collaboration and communication.

I have a two-part question for you, if I could. First, how frequently are you or your counterparts, your team members, how frequently are you in contact with these government agencies I mentioned above? Second, how has interagency coordination among these agencies strengthened or weakened pipeline security?

Mr. BLOUNT. Thank you for that question, Senator. We are in contact quite often with all the agencies that you mentioned. Again, as I noted, we are a regulated entity, and we know it is important to communicate what is going on across our pipeline system and with our operations, with all our governmental partners. And then there are a lot of entities within the government that do not regulate us, like CISA, up to May 7th, that we also have had constant communications going on.

I know from my CIO's perspective, she does spend a lot of time with CISA, she does spend a lot of time with the TSA talking about what is going on in cyberspace and defenses and things like that. I will go back to May 7th, and what I saw as being most helpful for an operator that has been, subject to an attack is, again, that was critical for us to be able to have that one central conduit in the government, and in this case it was DOE, who allowed us to communicate everything that was going on at the time through one central conduit, although all the parties that you mentioned were sitting at that table—virtually, of course, because of Coronavirus Disease (COVID)—hearing material real time that could help them go about doing their job or potentially could go about helping the market resolve the issue that we saw. So we saw a lot of permitting changes allowing truck drivers to drive longer hours or allowing trucks to carry more fuel. That was the kind of coordination that we go through that central conduit that the White House gave us.

Again, I am not saying one entity over the other. I am saying that the combination of all of them through that central conduit was extremely valuable to our response, extremely valuable to the American public to get as much fuel back into the system as we possibly could, and whether that is through deviations in regulations or things that allowed us to bring our pipeline on much sooner than perhaps it would have been.

Senator CARPER. Good. Maybe one other question. How quickly did your company reach out to the FBI?

Mr. BLOUNT. Senator, great question. We reached out to the FBI within hours.

Senator CARPER. What was the response?

Mr. BLOUNT. The response, Senator, was, "We want to get you back on a phone call. We are going to bring CISA into the conversation, and we are going to start going through it." I think part of that was we called the Atlanta office, and in this particular case, they felt it was DarkSide, and the FBI has an office specifically dedicated—they call it a "Center of Excellence"—for DarkSide, so their DarkSide experts, which are California based.

Again, as early as we called in the morning—I mean, I know the FBI probably responds regardless of the hour of the day. It was pretty early in California when we made our call to the Atlanta office. But great response on the part of the FBI.

Senator CARPER. Good. How about the response from CISA? That will be my last question. How about the response from CISA?

Mr. BLOUNT. Senator, of course, I was not involved in those conversations, but what I saw as a result of CISA being involved in those conversations was the ability to take some of the forensic evidence that the FBI was comfortable seeing released to the public wind up in CISA notifications that would then help like companies and certainly a lot of pipeline companies take a look at IPS addresses and things like that that we had shared during that phone call and get that out in memo form to other operators. So great sharing of information on the part of CISA.

Senator CARPER. Good. Thanks very much for joining us. Good luck.

Mr. BLOUNT. Thank you, sir.

Chairman PETERS. Thank you, Senator Carper.

Senator JOHNSON, you are recognized for your questions.

Opening Statement of Senator Johnson

Senator JOHNSON. Thank you, Mr. Chairman.
    I want to start out by again emphasizing and pointing out that you were the victim of a crime. You are not the bad guy here, and I appreciate my colleagues pretty well acknowledged that as well. I think that has been reflected in the line of questioning.
    I want to, because a lot of people do Monday morning quarterbacking and it is easy for Federal agencies to say, "No, do not pay ransoms because it just encourages more." But I just kind of want you to for the record lay out how much worse could it have been had you not made that very difficult decision to kind of bite the bullet so that you could get your pipelines back up and operational?
    Mr. BLOUNT. Senator, first, thank you for your kind words, and thank you for your question as well. That is an unknown we probably do not want to know, and it may be an unknown that we do not want to play out in a public forum. But if you start to look at the fact that it took us from Friday all the way to Wednesday afternoon the following, and we already started to see pandemonium going on in the markets, people doing unsafe things, like filling garbage bags full of gasoline or people fist-fighting in line at the fuel pump. The second would be what would happen if it had stretched on beyond that amount of time, right? What would happen at the airports where we supply a lot of jet fuel, let alone what might happen at the gas pump?
    My concern the first day was more to the first responders and the ambulances and the things that we count on in emergencies beyond our own current energy. That was my concern that first day. Again, our focus and our team's focus, regardless of what type of threat we see, is to identify the threat, contain the threat, remediate, and restore. And that goes beyond just an incident like that. That is about anything that we see is unsafe, and that is why the call that morning by that controller, the supervisor of the control room, to shut the pipeline down was so critical.
    Senator JOHNSON. I think that is an appropriate response, and I will leave it to people's imagination, but I want people thinking about that as well.
    Mr. BLOUNT. Yes, sir.
    Senator JOHNSON. Cyberattacks are an ongoing problem. There is no easy solution. As you say in your testimony, the criminals are on the offense, and they have a huge advantage. And it does not take much in terms of vulnerability—no matter how strong your IT systems are, your cybersecurity

systems are, there are vulnerabilities, and they get exploited, and they are becoming more and more susceptible to this.

In terms of government versus private sector, from my stand-point I think CISA is very valuable from the standpoint of sharing information preemptively, trying to stop some of these things. We have heard in testimony that 90 percent of these attacks can be prevented just by basic cyber hygiene. It certainly sounds like you had pretty sophisticated cyber hygiene, although obviously vulnerabilities.

The Federal Government can hold nation-states accountable that are allowing these cyberattackers to operate on their foreign soil and then, of course, hold them accountable when something happens, but also help in recovery and law enforcement.

I am not convinced that the Federal Government is going to be particularly effective at issuing standards and keeping them up-to-date. I really look to the private sector being far more nimble at that.

One of the processes I proposed is using a private sector model like an International Organization for Standardization (ISO) certification. I imagine you go through something like that. I did. You have six-month surveillance audits. You tie that to the insurance system as well where your rates are based on how good you achieve the standards. That is a system that will be as nimble as the private sector can be, as up-to-date, be able to employ the absolute best cybersecurity experts, which is one of the problems with the government. I am not—again, it is just a problem. Government cannot pay to retain the absolute best talent across the board.

I just kind of want your thoughts on that type of framework, public versus private.

Mr. BLOUNT. Senator, thank you, and I think those are all very good thoughts. I think, again, we have an obligation as a private entity to make sure that our systems are as capable as they possibly can be, and we have a responsibility to continue to look at those systems because, as we all know, the threat continues to evolve. The sophistication of the players continues to evolve. Their ability to compromise systems continually evolves. I think in combination with the government, together combined we have a much better ability as Americans to thwart the threat of cyberattacks, and I think that, again, we both have a responsibility. You shared the concept of private industry cannot do things to foreign governments, cannot put pressure on foreign governments. That is extremely important here if we look at where these criminals are housed, right? Something needs to be done there.

Again, I think that private-public partnership is very valuable, but we certainly know we have responsibilities and accountability as well.

Senator JOHNSON. Again, I am concerned about the government's, A, capability of establishing the standards, then, again, penalizing businesses for being victims of crime, if you do not meet their probably in many cases out-of-date standards. I would proceed down that line with caution.

Just real quick, were you a member of an Information Sharing and Analysis Center (ISAC), for your industry?

Mr. BLOUNT. Senator, I do not actually know the answer to that. If I can get back to you on——

Senator JOHNSON. OK. I would appreciate it.

Then the final question I have is: In our briefing and news reports, it was not just the shutdown, the ransomware. But prior to them shutting you down, they extracted all kinds of data that apparently they tend to reveal or not reveal. Can you describe that if possible? Because I am—"intrigued" is maybe the wrong word, but I thought that was quite interesting. Do you have any assurances—did you get that data back? Was that part of the ransom deal that that will not be disclosed? And can you tell us what kind of data they are talking about, why that would even be valuable for them or hurtful for that to be disclosed?

Mr. BLOUNT. Senator, very important question. As part of the ransomware note, they tell you that they have encrypted information, that they have exfiltrated information, so we knew that they had exfiltrated information. We worked very closely with the FBI on that, and the FBI is probably the best entity to respond to that since they are still, investigating the situation and getting closer, apparently, at least we hope, to the perpetrators themselves.

Senator JOHNSON. Would that be personal information from your employees that would be valuable or just trade secrets? I mean, you are a public company so the financial information is available. I am just kind of wondering what threat that represents to your entity or to your employees?

Mr. BLOUNT. Senator, what we know about that material right now is it was exfiltrated off the share drive, so it contains a lot of different type of material. The good news is it was retrieved very quickly. It was brought back in. Again, I think the FBI can talk a little bit more about that than I feel comfortable right now because of their investigation.

Senator JOHNSON. OK.

Mr. BLOUNT. But, again, the fact that it was retrieved very quickly is helpful. We do not fully understand everything that is in it because of where it has been held since it was retrieved. But we have people obviously involved in the combined process who have been looking very closely at that data.

Senator JOHNSON. OK. Listen, I appreciate you coming in here and being as forthright as you have become, so thank you.

Mr. BLOUNT. Thank you, Senator.

Chairman PETERS. Thank you, Senator Johnson.

Senator HASSAN, you are recognized for your questions.

Opening Statement of Senator Hassan[4]

Senator HASSAN. Thank you, Chair Peters, and thank you, Ranking Member Portman, for this hearing today. Thank you, Mr. Blount, for being willing to come before the Committee today.

Cybersecurity is a collaborative effort, to be sure, and we need to work together to strengthen public and private cyber defenses. Mr. Blount, I was glad to see that U.S. authorities were able to deprive hackers of millions of dollars in expected ransom. However, I want to better understand your decision to pay the ransom, and I understand it was a difficult decision.

As you have already discussed, the FBI and other Federal agencies strongly discourage paying ransom because it incentivizes more people to become cyber criminals and to develop better ransomware tools.

When you decided to pay the ransom, did you know how much of your network was affected at the time?

Mr. BLOUNT. Thank you for that question and good morning again.

Senator HASSAN. Good morning.

Mr. BLOUNT. No, we did not, and I think that is what a lot of people do not understand in these incidents, these attacks. It takes you days, basically, to see into your system that has been corrupted as to what you have, what has potentially been exfiltrated. In the case of Colonial, we had really good backups, is what I have been told by Mandiant. But it still took them days to get through those backups. When we look at our response time and ability to bring the system back up, it was fairly good in reality. My concern was you do not have that view at all for days, and when you have a critical asset like this, you have to focus on what is the best opportunity of options you have in front of you to take avail of, and in that case it was to get the encryption tool and to get our information back.

---

[4] The question of Senator Hassan appears in the Appendix.

Senator HASSAN. OK. I wanted to follow up. You mentioned the Federal agencies that you reached out to, but what, if any, outside of those agencies, non-Federal entities did you consult with? Were there private firms that you consulted with?

Mr. BLOUNT. Yes, Senator, great question. Obviously, we talked to Mandiant.

Senator HASSAN. Yes.

Mr. BLOUNT. We talked to Mandiant about that. We talked to our legal resources that have been involved in any number of cyber cases in the United States over the last couple years, people that have had real-time experience with these criminals as well as the specific science of cyberattacks and compromise. So, yes, a lot of conversation went into that decision that I made to negotiate.

Senator HASSAN. OK. Did you have a cybersecurity response plan in place prior to the attack? If so, did it include any guidance about paying a ransom?

Mr. BLOUNT. Senator, great question. What we have as a pipeline operator—and it would not be unique necessarily to us at Colonial—is we have an emergency response process.

Senator HASSAN. Right.

Mr. BLOUNT. Again, I said earlier this morning, see the threat, contain the threat, remediate the threat, and restore. So in this case, you use the same process, but you use a different set of experts. So in this case, we reached out immediately to the FBI because it was criminal.

Senator HASSAN. Right.

Mr. BLOUNT. We immediately reached out to legal resources that have dealt with this. We immediately reached out to Mandiant.

Senator HASSAN. Right, but my question is: In your planning, did you have a plan for cybersecurity response that included guidance about ransomware?

Mr. BLOUNT. Senator, specifically no discussion about ransom and action to ransom.

Senator HASSAN. Did your team do tabletop drills, for instance, to go through an actual simulated cyberattack before this happened?

Mr. BLOUNT. Senator, yes, we do participate in those with various groups, as well as do them on our own at Colonial.

Senator HASSAN. OK. Some private sector companies can focus strictly on economics and perform traditional cost-benefit analyses without having to consider national security concerns. However, owners and operators of critical infrastructure—and I appreciate your comments this morning acknowledging that Colonial oversees critical infrastructure. That carries a heightened obligation and duty to be capable of delivering goods and services to citizens in this case all up and down the East Coast.

Mr. Blount, Colonial Pipeline surely performed some number of cost-benefit analyses regarding the operation of its pipeline to determine how much to spend on pipeline hardware, personnel, and even cybersecurity. Did any of your analyses incorporate any public responsibility factors, such as the impact of a potential cyberattack on consumers or on the U.S. economy?

Mr. BLOUNT. Senator, that is a great question. I would not say that we approached it that way. We know our No. 1 goal at Colonial is to safely and securely operate that pipeline, because we have known for 57 years the importance of that pipeline to the well-being of the American citizen. So that has always been our focus. Our investment, whether it is in pipeline integrity or whether it is in cyberware and IT, is all derived around keeping safe and protecting the asset because of what its main benefit is to the United States.

Senator HASSAN. OK. I understand that, and I appreciate that answer. But, as you have had conversations with other Senators this morning, you have mentioned that you did not have two-step authentication in place. You have mentioned a legacy VPN which, in my understanding, means it was a pretty old VPN. I do not think it is acceptable to understand the critical nature of your product, but then not really have the preparation and the system in place to protect it as if it is critical infrastructure. You really do have an obligation to U.S. communities that you serve and to consumers and to our national security, so I am concerned that it does not seem to have been a formal factor in your analysis of how much to strengthen your systems.

Mr. BLOUNT. Senator, we take cybersecurity very seriously. I did reference earlier that the VPN was a legacy VPN——

Senator HASSAN. Yes.

Mr. BLOUNT [continuing]. That we could not see and it did not show up in any pen testing, that is unfortunate. But, again, the safety and the security of the system is highly critical. We have never had our board deny us any funds associated with safety and security, whether it is on the IT side or the physical side of the pipe. If my CIO wants funds, she gets them.

Senator HASSAN. OK. I would just—and this is an issue that I think we are seeing across the board on cyber. We need to start imagining what can happen and respond accordingly as opposed to always be looking at what the last problem was and really investing, and for critical infrastructure, I think it is absolutely important that we have standards that really make sure that companies are investing in the kind of infrastructure they need.

I have another question. I am running out of time, so I will submit it for the record.1 But I really would like to get your thoughts about what kind of public-private information sharing needs to happen, between and among whom, and at what level, because I think that is another important piece to this whole issue.

Thank you very much for being here this morning.

Thank you, Mr. Chair.

Chairman PETERS. Thank you, Senator Hassan, for your questions.

The Chair recognizes Senator LANKFORD for your questions.

Opening Statement of Senator Lankford

Senator LANKFORD. Thank you, Mr. Chairman.

Mr. Blount, thanks for being here. There is no CEO in America that wants to be sitting in the same chair you are sitting in right now, to be able to go through all this. You are a month past a major attack. Obviously, there is a lot of work that you are going through.

Can I back up for Colonial? When is the last time that the Colonial Pipeline was down and not providing fuel to the East Coast?

Mr. BLOUNT. Senator, that is a great question. That pipeline has never been down completely with the exception of—and I learned that just this week—over the couple hours of Y2K, and we can all appreciate going back in time that we were all concerned about the clock back then. Periodically from time to time we will have a portion of the system down during a hurricane event or something like that, but never the entire system at one time, and never for, obviously, that duration of time.

Senator LANKFORD. I think we as Americans get so used to going to the gas pump and filling up with refined products. Every one of us has landed at Charlotte airport and Jet A has been added to our plane as we change planes there. We get so used to that, we lost track of some of these things.

I want to ask a couple of things here. You had to do a physical inspection and a cyber inspection of this pipeline or just going through the digital portion of it, or physical inspection as well?

Mr. BLOUNT. Great question. So in the early hours of May 7th, we did not know exactly what we had. We had the ransomware. But, again, we are always concerned about the security of the pipeline, and you may have read in the press—and it is a factual statement. We drove over 29,000 miles of the pipeline, and, again, remember it is only a 5,500-mile pipeline. So we had constant ground surveillance. In addition, we also fly the pipeline—it is a PHMSA regulation that we fly the pipeline. We fly in excess of that regulation on a normal basis, and on top of that even doubled up our efforts during this point in time. Again, we did not know that it was just a cyberattack. We had to make sure that it was not potentially an attack on our physical structure as well.

Senator LANKFORD. So that was completed? There was no other physical damage that you could identify?

Mr. BLOUNT. That is correct, Senator. We did not see anything. We did keep an eye, obviously, on the pipeline. Just so you are aware, we kept the pipeline under pressure, and that would allow us to bring the pipeline up much quicker. So we had people manually in the field looking at gauges, the old-school way of watching pipeline pressures, to make sure that we were in compliance with all the regulations, regardless of the attack and what happened in the shutdown.

Senator LANKFORD. I said to several people that I have talked to in the last month, when we saw suddenly gas lines appearing and a pipeline go down at this point, that everyone learned the importance of pipelines. If I rewind two months before that, all the conversation was about, slowing down permitting new pipelines, maybe we are not going to do pipelines at all, make it harder to be able to do maintenance on Federal lands on pipelines. Two months ago, the conversation was, well, maybe we need fewer pipelines, and maybe we need to make this harder to be able to develop new pipelines—obviously, Keystone Pipeline was in the news—to say we are just not going to do that at all. And so products coming out of Canada and out of Montana are just going to have to find trucks and trains to be able to get there.

I am not going to ask you this same question because that is not going to be fair to you, but I have told a lot of folks what we watched happen with a sudden shutdown of a pipeline is the ghost of Christmas Future for the entire country if we do not continue to maintain our pipelines, increase capacity of pipelines, if we do not continue to expand and have duplication of pipelines in spots, to be able to make sure we have redundancy for this. Pipelines are essential to America. The 2.5 million miles of pipelines that we have scattered around the country, we lost track of how incredibly important they are.

I am grateful that your company has had such a good reputation. This is terrible to be a victim of a ransomware attack. There is something that you have that every CEO in America would like to hear, and that is, what are the lessons learned on cyber issues that you have already identified, obviously your team has taken on? The No. 1 has already come out, looking for legacy entries into your system that do not have two-factor authentication on it. What else has been identified that you need to be able to take and pass on to others?

Mr. BLOUNT. Thank you for your question. Again, I think the most important thing is to not be complacent about what you have because of the pace of change on the outside, from the criminal side. And then secondary to that, but equally as important, is the ability to have an emergency response process in place. If we had not been trained for the last 57 years to respond to any threat, whatever that threat is—it is an extension cord on the ground that has not been taped down that someone might trip over and hurt themselves— if we had not been trained like that and our employees had not been trained like that, who knows how many days it potentially could have taken to bring the asset back online? We know the importance of the asset. We are dedicated to the American public as a result of all the training and everything that we have done through the years to make sure that we have the fuel that we need.

Senator LANKFORD. Backing up systems, clearing unused accountable, guarding data in other ways. Are there other things that you would mention to say these are lessons that are going to be important for the future? Obviously, there was a gap, a single area, a single vulnerability. Other lessons you would mention?

Mr. BLOUNT. Thank you, Senator. I think from a proactive standpoint, you have seen now where we brought Mandiant in to investigate as well as to restore and start to harden our systems. But we have talked a lot about standards in this room today, and so we have also brought Dragos in and Black Hills in, and people may ask why, is that overkill? I would say I do not think so because what we want to make sure is we get the best out of each one of those experts. They all have a specific skill. Dragos is very good at operational technology (OT) systems. We want to make sure that we have the best hardening and the best segmentation we can possibly have on our OT side.

So I think, again, it is that investment in resources to get the best in class, because, again, even the best in class is still susceptible. We have heard that from each one of those experts.

Senator LANKFORD. All right. So this is not a ransomware attack. This is actually somebody that is getting into the system. Have you been able to determine going through it whether they would be able to get your operating system to be able to change pressure, to be able to change volume, to be able to change flow through the structure that actually came through?

Mr. BLOUNT. Senator, that is a great question. Obviously, that factored in largely to my decision and the employees' decision to shut the pipeline down that day. We did not know, and we probably did not know the answer to that for days. The investigation is ongoing. But up to this point, Mandiant has not confirmed any evidence that they were in the OT system, and typically that is not what DarkSide does.

Senator LANKFORD. Right, it is a different animal, but it is a vulnerability that sits out there for someone else that does mean to be able to do our Nation harm, not just your company harm, at this point, and they are not just going out for money, but they are actually going out for physical damage. Thanks for being here. Thanks for being so frank in your testimony.

Mr. BLOUNT. Thank you, Senator.

Chairman PETERS. Thank you, Senator LANKFORD.

Senator ROSEN, you are now recognized for your questions.

Opening Statement of Senator Rosen

Senator ROSEN. Thank you, Chairman Peters, Ranking Member Portman. This hearing, of course, is so timely, so important. Mr. Blount, thank you so much for spending your time with us today to bring some clarity to these extremely important issues to our Nation, because you know what? It is a challenge for business owners across a variety of industries to commit the resources necessary and critical to preventing and combating cyber threats. It requires a team of dedicated staff with cyber expertise and the technologies needed actually to defend against an attack.

Mr. Blount, it would be helpful to understand the resources you have at Colonial Pipeline devoted to cybersecurity technology personnel and trainings. So can you tell us just a bit about your cyber guidelines and best practices your company follows? Do you collaborate with Federal agencies like National Institute of Standards and Technology (NIST), DOE, and CISA? If you do not, why not? And just talk about your plans, either current collaboration or collaboration going forward, if you plan to do that.

Mr. BLOUNT. Thank you, Senator, for that very important question. We are highly collaborative organization. We are highly transparent organization. We spent a lot of time in Washington, at least up until COVID, and now we spend a lot of time on the phone and in Zoom calls with all our regulators as well as other entities like CISA, like the DOE, and other people that we feel accountable to for what we do for the Nation.

Again, very communicative, very present in Washington with all the Federal agencies that we have access to, and we certainly appreciate all the collaboration that we are able to do with them. From a Colonial perspective, we have over 100 people dedicated to IT. Our CIO, when she asks for funds related to anything associated with cyber, she gets it. Our board is highly supportive of anything that protects the pipeline and protects our data. So we have never had any issue from the standpoint of getting the funding that we need in order to protect the asset and to protect our information and protect the American public.

Senator ROSEN. Thank you. I want to kind of build on this a little bit because, according to recent news reports, you have discussed scheduling a voluntary cybersecurity review with TSA. A lot of people have touched on this. But that review never took place, and so how often does your company conduct internal cybersecurity reviews or self-assessments? Do you do this on a regular schedule? And what do you do with the results? Who do you share them with, or do you share them?

Mr. BLOUNT. Senator, thank you for that question. With regard to the Validated Architecture Design Review (VADR) voluntary program that TSA has, I had also heard in the press that we had refused to participate in that, and that was quite a shock to me and quite a shock to our CIO. We maintain a lot of conversation with the TSA and specifically the Director of Security level there. We have participated in any number of things with the TSA in the past, including physical screening of our facilities. We have actually had the head of TSA in our office meeting with me and my management team.

Senator ROSEN. Do you do your own internal reviews? Do you share them with others? Do you do those on a regular basis? I guess that is also the point of my question as well.

Mr. BLOUNT. Senator, we do participate in periodic penetration tests. We do auditing, outside auditing of our cyber procedures and our IT department. And like all audits, you expect you are going to find something with the pace of change outside from the threat, and you rank the things that come back, and then you go about the business of tackling those things that are deemed deficient or weak in order to improve your defenses. So, yes, we do.

Senator ROSEN. I want to build on that because you have repeatedly said during this hearing that you were not part of conversations in the wake of the cyberattack, including the discussion with the FBI about paying a ransom. In hindsight, if you are doing this analysis, you are ranking things, doing all this, do you think you should have been part of those conversations?

Mr. BLOUNT. Senator, that is a very good question. This was an all-hands-on-deck day and week. My responsibility that week was to communicate to my board, make sure that my team was communicating where they needed to communicate. I directly handled all the discussions at the DOE level, including the daily briefings that we did with the DOE. I participated in the briefing with the Governor's offices throughout the States that were impacted. So while it would be nice to be involved in every conversation, the reality of it is I cannot be every place at once, but it was well taken care of by any number of my management team members, the people that report directly to me.

Senator ROSEN. Thank you. I appreciate that.

I want to talk a little bit about my Cyber Sense Act because we know, of course, cyberattacks, that is what has happened to you. So last Congress I introduced the Cyber Sense Act. It is bipartisan legislation that would create a voluntary cyber sense program at the Department of Energy that is going to test the cybersecurity of products and technologies intended for use in our bulk power system. This bill also directs the Energy Secretary to consider incentives to encourage the use of analysis and testing results when designing products and technologies, although I think the incentive would actually be not to be hacked.

But, Mr. Blount, while the program my bill would establish is solely for electric utilities, do you think a similar program for pipelines would be helpful for gas companies like yours across the board to collaborate and communicate and have some sense of what is going on in the industry?

Mr. BLOUNT. Senator, thank you for that question. I think that is a great program for the electric utilities, and I think anything that would help our side of the business be more secure and less susceptible to any threats is a great idea.

Senator ROSEN. Thank you. I think the last question—I have about a minute left—I just want to ask a quick question about why Colonial Pipeline did not notify CISA immediately following the ransomware attack. Mr. Wales told this Committee "there is benefit when CISA is brought in quickly, because of the information we glean, we work to share it in a broader fashion to protect other critical infrastructure."

So what is your response to Mr. Wales' statement and you not sharing your ransomware attack?

Mr. BLOUNT. I am glad you asked that question, Senator. One of the first phone calls we made that morning within hours of noticing the compromise was to the FBI office, and during that conversation with the FBI, the FBI said,

"We will call you back later. We want to bring in our Center of Excellence from California into the conversation, and we will call CISA and bring them into the conversation." So at that point, based upon the number of phone calls that we had to make that day to any number of governmental entities, we knew that CISA would be notified and brought into the conversation. We had a conversation with CISA the first day as a result of that connection with the FBI. If the FBI had not called them, we would have. We called every other governmental agency we were required to and then some that day.

Again, I do not know why he made that statement, but I can tell you we would have called him. There is no reason not to. We were extremely transparent, and we wanted all the help that we could get that morning.

Senator ROSEN. Thank you very much for your testimony today. My time has expired, Mr. Chairman.

Chairman PETERS. Thank you, Senator Rosen.

Senator HAWLEY, you are recognized for your questions.

Opening Statement of Senator Hawley[5]

Senator HAWLEY. Thank you, Mr. Chairman.

Thank you, Mr. Blount, for being here.

I think you mentioned this in your written testimony, but I would just like to start here. What percentage approximately of all fuel on the East Coast of the United States is transported by your company's pipeline?

Mr. BLOUNT. Thank you for that question, Senator. It is approximately 45 percent.

Senator HAWLEY. How many gallons of fuel does your company's pipeline transport on a daily basis?

Mr. BLOUNT. Normally we would move approximately 100 million gallons of fuel a day, Senator.

Senator HAWLEY. That is a lot. Is it fair to say that tens of millions of Americans do not really have any choice but to rely on your pipeline for fuel? You have enormous market power, is what I am driving at. Is that a fair statement?

Mr. BLOUNT. Senator, over time we have evolved as a big player in the fuel business, and it is because of our reliability record and, quite frankly, we are the cheapest cost of transportation for the fuel to those customers.

---

[5] The information requested by Senator Hawley appears in the Appendix.

Senator HAWLEY. Yes, I think that the amount of fuel running through the pipeline exceeds the fuel consumption of Germany. If I am not mistaken, the closure of your pipeline facilitated nearly— or led to nearly 16,000 gas stations without fuel across the country, which is huge. You are huge, and consumers really rely on your, is my point.

I am curious as to, given this, given your market power, given the reliance of consumers, given the sheer number of consumers you serve, why didn't you take up the Transportation Security Administration's offer to do a comprehensive cybersecurity review of the pipeline?

Mr. BLOUNT. Senator, thank you for asking that question. We indeed were in contact with them about setting that up. Obviously, COVID got in the way in the early days of that. We were getting ready to move at the end of the year into a new facility, so I think the conversation was that we want to do it, the VADR program is a good program, but we will schedule that later on. We do have that scheduled at the end of July.

Senator HAWLEY. So it was a COVID issue, basically? Or it was a moving issue, you were moving to a new headquarters? I am looking at the Washington Post article here that reports that the TSA had tried to schedule a voluntary in-depth cybersecurity review but that Colonial just could not get it done. Any regret not doing that in retrospect?

Mr. BLOUNT. Senator, anything that you could do is always helpful. If we look at that test, it is a great test, but it is not dissimilar to a lot of the tests that we already do in our system. Again, we have a good working relationship with TSA. I am a little surprised by the statement that I heard about refusal, actually investigated it on my end from my CIO and their contacts on the TSA side. No one really understood why the word "refused" was used.

Senator HAWLEY. So just let me understand your last statement. Are you saying you think that the TSA review would have been redundant, not particularly helpful? You said it is duplicative of things you do on your own end internally.

Mr. BLOUNT. Senator, I think in this case it probably would not have resulted in finding that legacy VPN. Again, they do not actually go into the system. It is a questionnaire format type thing. I am not saying it would not be valuable. It very much could be. I think each one of these tests are slightly different, so if there is that one little piece that can make the difference in seeing something, that is helpful. Again, never any issue with us actually getting to the point of doing that. It was a timing issue.

Senator HAWLEY. Got you. Who owns Colonial Pipeline?

Mr. BLOUNT. Colonial Pipeline is owned by several entities.

Senator HAWLEY. Including?

Mr. BLOUNT. Including a division of Shell, Midstream actually, Caisse du Quebec, KKR, IFM, and Koch Industries.

Senator HAWLEY. Got it. I am asking that because it has been reported that over the last decade Colonial has distributed—I am looking at the article here from Bloomberg. Colonial has distributed almost all of your profits, sometimes more, actually, in the form of dividends to your investors. In 2018, for instance, Colonial Pipeline paid $670 million to its owners, which actually exceeded your net income for that year. That is a pretty good return. What do you invest in cybersecurity every year?

Mr. BLOUNT. That is a great question, Senator. We invested over $200 million over the last five years in our IT systems.

Senator HAWLEY. And that is cybersecurity? How about on an annual basis for cybersecurity? $670 million distributed in dividends in 2018 alone, give me a sense of—you are operating not unlike a public utility, right? I mean, we covered the fact you serve 45, 50 percent of customers on the East Coast; you transport 100 million gallons a day. The attack on you led to 16,000 gas stations being shut down. So just give me a sense of—given the importance of your company, the size of it, the reliance, what are you doing in terms of your investment for cybersecurity? I know you are paying your investors well.

Mr. BLOUNT. Yes, Senator, great question. Our dividend policy is not much different than any other Midstream company, so I want to state that first. Our owners have never denied us any opportunity to spend what we need to spend in order to keep the pipeline safe and secure.

Senator HAWLEY. Which is about what a year?

Mr. BLOUNT. Take the average, over $200 million in the last five years.

Senator HAWLEY. OK, I tell you what——

Mr. BLOUNT. Over $1.5 billion in system integrity every five years.

Senator HAWLEY. Got it. We will give you this as a question for the record so that we can get the actual—I know you do not have the number right in front of you, but we will give you the question for the record,1 and you can give us the exact number on an annual basis. I think that would be interesting to know.

You talk about Federal regulations in your testimony, and you say Congress should consider designating an official point of contact at a Federal agency to better facilitate communications. That is an interesting idea. What rules do you think Congress ought to consider requiring of you and your company? So your suggestion is what the Federal Government should do itself, but given, again, your status, given the reliance on you, what do you think Congress ought to require of your company and companies like it going forward?

Mr. BLOUNT. Senator, great question. I think what Congress should require is that we have a focus on safety and security of this critical asset, and I think we have demonstrated that over the last 57 years of responsible ownership and operations.

Senator HAWLEY. Let me ask you a little bit about the attack in the IT system. I understand that the attack occurred or was first detected only in the IT network, not in the OT network. Is that right? Do I have that correct?

Mr. BLOUNT. Senator, that is correct.

Senator HAWLEY. OK.

Mr. BLOUNT. That is what the investigation shows up to this point.

Senator HAWLEY. Got it. OK. So, to your knowledge, the OT network, the operational technology network, would not have been compromised by the attack if you had not shut down—you shut that down as a precaution, security measure?

Mr. BLOUNT. Senator, if there was one percent chance that that OT system was compromised, it was worth shutting the pipeline system down.

Senator HAWLEY. Got it. I am just trying to establish that, to your knowledge, at this time you think it was concentrated in the IT system?

Mr. BLOUNT. Senator, based upon the investigation by me——

Senator HAWLEY. Got it.

Mr. BLOUNT [continuing]. Up to this point, that would be a correct statement.

Senator HAWLEY. Yes, OK. This leads me to ask this. The pipeline is seven years old, roughly, right? There was a time, I assume—and you correct me if I am wrong, but there was a time, I assume, where you operated the pipeline without today's computer systems. What I am driving toward here is do you have the capability to manually operate the pipeline in the future in the event of an IT attack like this one? If you do not have that capability, should you, do you think, going forward?

Mr. BLOUNT. Senator, that is a great question. We actually did operate small portions of the pipeline manually in order to alleviate some of the fuel shortage, and the discussion took place with the operations team about the ability to do that systemwide. And the response to that was it would be quicker to get back up on our feet by correcting the corruption of the critical IT systems that we needed in order to get the pipeline system up and operate it manually. But I think on a go-forward basis, there is no question that we will look at that capability, and it is a really interesting question because if you look at the aging workforce now, a lot of those people that did operate Colonial Pipeline and other infrastructure in America historically manually, they are retiring or they are gone. Fortunately, we still have that last bit of that generation which allowed us to do what we did during this particular event. It is a great question.

Senator HAWLEY. Very good. Thank you for being here. Thank you, Mr. Chairman.

Chairman PETERS. Thank you, Senator Hawley.
Senator OSSOFF, you are recognized for your questions.

Opening Statement of Senator Ossoff

Senator OSSOFF. Thank you, Mr. Chairman. Thank you as well to Ranking Member Portman. Mr. Blount, thank you for being here today. Thank you for your candid testimony. I want to express my appreciation to your team based in Georgia for their diligent efforts to restore service swiftly and offer you the opportunity before the Committee now to state any lessons learned as well as reflections on potential improvements to Federal policy that we have not had a chance yet to explore on the record.

I also want to thank you for your team's continual updates of my team as you sought to restore service, as you have investigated the nature of the threat, and for the conversation that you and I have had about the matter as well. But lessons learned, recommendations for Congress.

Mr. BLOUNT. Good morning, Senator.
Senator OSSOFF. Good morning.
Mr. BLOUNT. Thank you for your kind words, too. Yes, I think there are several really important lessons learned. I think, the most important lesson learned is to respond immediately, right? We have talked about stop-work authority at Colonial, the ability to identify the threat, contain the threat, remediate the threat, and restart the system. Again, that goes toward any type of threat that we see, not just particularly a cyber threat. I think that is an important thing for any operator to remember, is contain that threat. The other side that I would like to share with you that I think is extremely important is communication, and there has been a lot of conversation in this room about who did you talk to and who did you communicate with and at what time did you do that. I will stress again I think that what we learned was that being transparent and responding quickly and not being afraid to come forward was

probably one of the most important things that we did in this particular case, not foreign to us but perhaps foreign to others.

Finally, I would add I think the ability to communicate with the Federal Government through one conduit, regardless of who it is, was extremely valuable to us because, again, as I looked at this all- hands-on-deck effort that we had to do, the ability to communicate everything that we were seeing, whether it was the market response or the things that we were trying to get done on the IT side to do the restart all the way to the investigative side of the equation, extremely helpful for a management team already stretched to be able to communicate quickly and efficiently, and then allow our government partners to do what they could do to help us, which indeed they did. They were very helpful in the process.

Senator OSSOFF. Thank you, Mr. Blount. As you and I discussed last week, your team, I believe in collaboration with Mandiant, is conducting a comprehensive review of the threat, the nature of the attack, what might have been done to mitigate the risk, the efforts to thwart the attack once it was discovered. Is that correct?

Mr. BLOUNT. Yes, Senator, that is correct.

Senator OSSOFF. What impediment would there be, if any, to sharing the results of that review and the conclusions of that investigation, including at the technical level with this Committee once it is completed?

Mr. BLOUNT. Senator, I do not think there are any issues with that. What we have been trying to do all along the way is share the information as we learn it. We have been very straightforward about the legacy VPN. Hopefully that will help out other operators who have similar type legacy assets.

We know from working with Mandiant that is not an unusual issue for companies. I think we will continue to communicate as we go through the process with Mandiant, but our ability and desire to sit down with you is ready and available when you would like that.

Senator OSSOFF. Great. So we can expect that once that review and investigation are complete, you would voluntarily share with this Committee the results of Mandiant's investigation?

Mr. BLOUNT. Yes, Senator, we will be very transparent.

Senator OSSOFF. I appreciate that. When you and I spoke last week, I believe you stated that you had not refused any requests for information from the Department of Homeland Security, the FBI, or other Federal entities. You have discussed the importance of the free flow of information between the target of an attack like this and the Federal Government.

Having now had the experience of your company being subjected to an attack such as this and the communication that you had to engage in swiftly with Federal entities, what do you think can be done to improve and make more efficient and direct the flow of information between the victim of a cyberattack and Federal law enforcement, Federal cybersecurity authorities? I want to drill down a little bit on the following: You and I also discussed last week that the criminal enforcement side of the investigation and the cybersecurity side of the investigation overlap but are also distinct. Have you found any difference in the quality of the Federal response, the nature of the communication with Federal authorities between the criminal prosecutorial investigation and the cybersecurity investigation?

Mr. BLOUNT. Senator, from my perspective, I would say the answer is no. Again, as we discussed, we had FBI, CISA, and, of course, Mandiant helping in the process. We told Mandiant from the very beginning if the FBI had questions or CISA had questions, please share information with them. Of course, as structured by the White House, we had the ability to communicate with everybody else on the restoration side and on the supply concern side through the DOE. Again, that worked wonderfully for us. Again, our time was stretched during the day when we were trying to respond to the situation and get things remediated so that we could bring the pipeline back up. From my perspective as the CEO, to sit down at least at 5 p.m. every day and sometimes more often phone calls would come, but at least have the ability to communicate, the restoration side, what we were doing to restore the IT systems, share market intelligence because we have a unique perspective as Colonial as well. That was very helpful.

So regardless of who that conduit is, the ability to communicate on the investigative side with all those parties at once and on the restoration and the market side, extremely valuable to us. As you can imagine, there is a lot going on as you head toward bringing an asset like this back up, and you have a lot of people that want to know a lot of things, and you do not have all the answers yet. But what I found is by having them all in the same room, the expert on this one particular area would say, "They would not know that yet," and that would alleviate a lot of concern that the less knowledgeable person might have, even though they were very strong in what their particular discipline or science was.

Senator OSSOFF. Thank you, Mr. Blount. Finally, circling back to the ongoing Mandiant investigation, can you commit that the product that you share with this Committee of that investigation will be the same product that you and your executive team and your board review and that it will not be a different set of conclusions that are produced for the consumption of Congress but it will be the same assessment that you receive?

Mr. BLOUNT. Senator, as I have stated previously, we will be very transparent. I think the one thing that we need to be careful about as a Nation is how do we share that information. Obviously, it would be very difficult in a public forum like this because a lot of what we will share about our strengthening and hardening of our systems will be critical to keeping those strong and defensive against attacks.

But, yes, we need to talk and figure out what is the best way to talk about what happened as well as what best practice on a goforward basis is for an operator like ours that operates such sensitive infrastructure.

Senator OSSOFF. So recognizing that some of those conclusions, information, and plans may be sensitive and confidential, nevertheless the appropriate forum for those confidences being provided, we will be able to exchange that information freely and review in full the Mandiant report?

Mr. BLOUNT. Senator, we will gladly cooperate with you.

Senator OSSOFF. Thank you, Mr. Blount.

I yield back, Mr. Chairman.

Chairman PETERS. Thank you, Senator Ossoff.

Mr. Blount, I would like to thank you for joining us here this morning on this incredibly important matter. We are clearly experiencing relentless and unprecedented assaults against both our private and public sector information systems, and we are getting those assaults by both criminal organization as well as foreign adversaries, and this is a grave national security concern. Certainly from the questions that were posed today by all of my colleagues, I think it is clear that my colleagues believe this is something that we need to address immediately and in a comprehensive fashion. It is clear to me that the cyberattack against Colonial highlights the need for increased cooperation and coordination between both the Federal Government and our critical infrastructure partners. We must ensure that the American people are capable of not only defending our critical infrastructure partners from attack, but also maintaining a secure information system environment to prevent those cyberattacks from occurring in the first place.

The interference that American lives depend on is increasingly connected, connected to each other and connected to the Internet. This brings a whole new meaning to the phrase "You are only as strong as your weakest link," and these weak links can be hacked accounts, inadequate passwords, or unknown vulnerabilities to the system.

More must be done in this space, and I am committed to certainly focusing my attention. I think every Member on this Committee agrees that this Committee will focus our collective attention and resources on dealing with this problem. Cyberattacks used to be merely an inconvenience. We now know that they are becoming attacks on our very way of life.

Once again, thank you for appearing here today. I look forward to your continued engagement on this important issue.

The record for this hearing will remain open for 15 days, until June 23rd at 5 p.m., for submission of statements and questions for the record.

With that, this hearing is now adjourned.

[Whereupon, at 11:33 a.m., the Committee was adjourned.]

Appendix

Chairman Peters Opening Statement as Prepared for Delivery

Mr. Blount, welcome to the Committee. Thank you for joining us for this important discussion on the harmful cyber-attack against your company, Colonial Pipeline, and how we can work to strengthen coordination and response to these serious cybersecurity incidents.

When Colonial Pipeline was forced to shut down operations last month due to a ransomware attack, millions of Americans up and down the East Coast had their lives disrupted by gas shortages and price increases.

In the weeks since your company was struck, we have seen a series of other attacks, on everything from our transportation networks to meat-packing centers. Those private sector strikes follow especially damaging attacks on our government, including the extensive SolarWinds hack last year.

While the objectives of these attacks differ, they all demonstrate that bad actors, whether criminal organizations or foreign governments, are always looking to exploit the weakest link, infiltrate networks, steal information, and disrupt American life.

Mr. Blount, I am glad your company continues to recover from this malicious attack and that the FBI was able to recover millions of dollars in ransom paid. But I am alarmed that this breach ever occurred, and that communities from Texas to New York suffered as a result.

I appreciate that you have joined us today, to provide answers to the Committee and the American people on how a group of criminals was able to infiltrate your networks – steal nearly 100 gigabytes of data in just two hours – and then lock your systems with ransomware to demand payment. I am also looking forward to hearing an update on your progress to recover from this serious breach.

Private entities, especially those that are critical to our nation's infrastructure, are responsible for assessing their individual risk and investing in the technology to prevent breaches and ensure they can continue providing service to customers who rely on them for basic necessities, like fuel.

At the same time, the federal government must develop a comprehensive, all of government approach to not only defend against cyber-attacks, but punish foreign adversaries who continue to perpetuate them or harbor criminal organizations that target American systems.

This approach requires bolstering our defenses, and using the full might of our diplomatic, military, and intelligence capabilities.

We must also ensure private entities, like Colonial, are providing the federal government with timely and relevant information in the event of major incidents.

We need federal agencies charged with cybersecurity – like the Department of Homeland Security and the Cybersecurity and Infrastructure Security Agency – to understand the extent of these attacks and how best to support victims.

Make no mistake – if we do not step up our cybersecurity readiness – the consequences will be severe. The ransomware attack on Colonial Pipeline affected millions of Americans. The next time an incident like this happens – it could be even worse.

As Chairman of this Committee – I am committed to prioritizing policies that will help secure our critical infrastructure networks – including in the proposed infrastructure package Congress is negotiating.

Protecting the American people from these sophisticated – harmful – and growing attacks will not be easy. We must learn from our past mistakes – find out what went wrong – and work together to tackle this enormous challenge. Inaction, however, is NOT an option.

OPENING STATEMENT
RANKING MEMBER ROB PORTMAN
THREATS TO CRITICAL INFRASTRUCTURE: EXAMINING THE COLONIAL PIPELINE CYBERATTACK

June 8, 2021

Thank you, Chairman Peters. I've appreciated our bipartisan work over the years to improve cybersecurity and I look forward to continuing our partnership.

Today's topic is both incredibly relevant and highly concerning: ransomware attacks on critical infrastructure. Ransomware paralyzes a company by locking its computer systems and holding its data and operations hostage until the ransom is paid. Increasingly, ransomware hackers pursue a two pronged ransom approach where they also download and threaten to release sensitive victim data.

There seems to be a new ransomware attack every week. While today, we will hear from a recent ransomware victim, Colonel Pipeline, these attacks are not limited to one sector. No entity – public or private – is safe from these attacks.

Last week, we learned that ransomware shut down the world's largest meat processor, JBS, including nine beef plants in the United States. Both the Colonial Pipeline attack and the JBS attacks were attributed to Russian criminal organizations.

Just this morning, news broke that a constituent outreach services platform that nearly 60 offices in the House of Representatives use was hit with a ransomware attack. As I said before, no one is safe from these attacks.

I hope today's hearing will cover four topics:

First, we must understand that these attacks have real-world consequences.

- On May 7, Colonial Pipeline learned they suffered a ransomware attack impacting their information technology, or IT, systems by DarkSide, a Russia-based criminal group.

- Recent news reports indicate that hackers accessed Colonial's systems through a compromised password of a Virtual Private Network account.

- This account did not use multifactor authentication, a basic cybersecurity best practice, which easily allowed the hackers to gain access.

- Colonial moved quickly to disconnect their operational systems to prevent hackers from moving laterally and accessing those systems.

- This was an appropriate response to a cyberattack, but it made Colonial's critical pipelines unusable. And that is a huge problem—Colonial Pipeline provides about 45 percent of the East Coast's fuel.

- With operations shut down, people across the East Coast bought fuel in a panic, unsure how long the shortage would last.

- Colonial brought its systems back online within a week, easing what could have been a much worse situation.

Second, this shows the difficult decision ransomware victims face: should they pay the ransom or not?

- The U.S. government, including both CISA and the FBI, strongly recommend organizations do not pay ransoms.

- Paying ransoms rewards ransomware hackers—if no one paid ransoms, criminals would have little incentive to engage in ransomware attacks.

- And even if an entity pays, there is no guarantee that the hackers will give them the decryption key or not strike again.

- However, organizations must weigh these consequences against keeping their operations offline—in this case, limiting 45 percent of the East Coast's fuel supply.

- Colonial Pipeline paid DarkSide a ransom of 75 bitcoins—worth over $4 million at the time. Yesterday, the Department of Justice announced the recovery of 63.7 of those bitcoins, but DOJ won't always be able to recover those ransom payments.

- I appreciate Mr. Blount's transparency in acknowledging that his company paid the $4.4 million ransom. I hope today we can explore the reasons for that decision.

Third, this attack demonstrates the gaps in information sharing between impacted organizations and the federal government.

- Last month, Brandon Wales, the Acting Director of CISA, testified in response to one of my questions that he didn't think Colonial Pipeline would have contacted CISA at all if the FBI didn't bring them in.

- CISA's authorities allow the agency to engage on a voluntary basis, when requested by an affected organization. While I think this is the right approach, CISA must have relevant information to be able to share it among other critical infrastructure owners and operators who may be similarly targeted.

Finally, we must recognize these ransomware attacks for what they are: a severe national security threat.

- Attacks against critical infrastructure entities are not just attacks on companies; they are attacks on our country itself.

- When DarkSide attacked Colonial Pipeline, it wasn't just the company that was affected. Americans across the East Coast felt the squeeze at fuel pumps when Colonial shut off nearly 50 percent of the fuel supply.

- The criminals conducting these attacks often operate with at least the tacit acceptance of the foreign countries they operate out of. The U.S. Government needs to take stronger steps to hold those countries, like Russia, accountable.

Ransomware attacks will continue to plague U.S. companies and critical infrastructure. As the committee of jurisdiction over both cybersecurity and critical infrastructure security, we need to reevaluate how we defend against ransomware, and identify solutions to mitigate the consequences of these attacks.

Hearing Before the United States Senate Committee on Homeland Security & Governmental Affairs June 8, 2021

Testimony of Joseph Blount, President and Chief Executive Officer Colonial Pipeline Company

I. Introduction

Chairman Peters, Ranking Member Portman, and Members of the Committee: My name is Joe Blount, and since late 2017, I have served as the President and Chief Executive Officer of Colonial Pipeline Company. Thank you for the opportunity to testify before the Committee today.

The Colonial Pipeline Company was founded in 1962 and is proud of its long history of connecting refineries with customers throughout the Southern and Eastern United States. Today, we have about 950 employees across the United States. Colonial Pipeline is the largest refined products pipeline by volume in the country and transports many products, such as gasoline, diesel, aviation fuels, and home heating oil. Our pipeline system is one of the most complex pieces of infrastructure in America, if not the world. On any given day, we may transport more than 100 million gallons of product. Shipping that product is what we do. We do not own the fuel, the refineries, the marketers or gas stations. Rather, we transport it from 29 refineries in the Gulf Coast all the way up to the New York Harbor.

Colonial Pipeline is cognizant of the important role we play as critical infrastructure. We recognize our significance to the economic and national security of the United States and know that disruptions in our operations can have serious consequences. Our pipeline system spans more than 5,500 miles.

The product we transport accounts for nearly half of the fuel consumed on the East Coast, providing energy for more than 50 million Americans. Not only do everyday Americans rely on our pipeline operations to get fuel at the pump, but so do cities and local governments, to whom we supply fuel for critical operations, such as airports, ambulances and first responders.

The safety and security of our pipeline system is something we take very seriously, and we operate with the interests of our customers, shippers and country top of mind.

Just one month ago, we were the victims of a ransomware attack by the cyber-criminal group DarkSide. At this time, we believe the criminal attack encrypted our IT systems, and DarkSide demanded a financial payment in exchange for a key to unlock those systems. We responded swiftly to the attack itself and to the disruption that the attack caused. We were in a harrowing situation and had to make difficult choices that no company ever wants to face, but I am proud of the fact that our people reacted quickly to get the pipeline back up and running safely. I am also extraordinarily grateful for the immediate and sustained support of federal law enforcement and governmental authorities, including the White House. We reached out to federal authorities within hours of the attack and since that time we have found them to be true allies as we've worked to quickly and safely restore and secure our operations. We also look forward to their support as the United States enhances its response to the increasing challenges private companies must address in light of the proliferation of ransomware attacks and the actions of these cyber-criminal groups.

I appreciate your interest in this incident and our response, and I welcome the opportunity to discuss it with you. Our hope is that we will all learn from what happened and, through sharing, develop even more robust tools and intelligence to address this threat moving forward.

I also want to express my gratitude to the employees of Colonial Pipeline, our numerous partners, and the American people for their actions and support as we responded to the attack and dealt with the disruption that it caused. We are deeply sorry for the impact that this attack had, but are heartened by the resilience of our country and of our company.

II. Timeline of the Morning of the Ransomware Attack

We identified the ransomware attack just before 5:00 AM Eastern Daylight Time (EDT) on Friday, May 7th, when one of our employees identified the ransom note on a system in the IT network.

Shortly after learning of the attack, the employee notified the Operations Supervisor at our Control Center who put in the stop work order to halt operations throughout the pipeline. This decision was driven by the imperative to isolate and contain the attack to help ensure the malware did not spread to the Operational Technology (OT) network, which controls our pipeline operations, if it had not already. At approximately 5:55 AM EDT, employees began the shutdown process. By 6:10 AM EDT, they confirmed that all 5,500 miles of pipelines had been shut down. Overall, it took us approximately fifteen minutes to close down the conduit, which has about 260 delivery points across 13 states and Washington, D.C. On May 7, our employees activated our company-wide incident response process and executed the steps they were trained to carry out. Shutting down the pipeline was absolutely the right decision, and I stand by our employees' decision to do what they were trained to do.

We have an incident response process that follows the same framework used by some federal agencies. Everyone in the company—from me to the operators in the field—has stop work authority if they believe that the safety of our systems is at risk, and that is a critical part of our incident response process.

I recognize that the attackers were able to access our systems. While that never should have happened, it is a sobering fact that we cannot change. That being said, I am proud and grateful to report that our response worked: we were able to quickly identify, isolate, and respond to the attack and stop the malware from spreading and causing even more damage. We then turned to remediating the problem and safely restoring service. We retained a leading forensic firm, Mandiant, and with their help, within hours, we were able to return some of our local lines to manual operation. Within days, we returned all of our lines to operation. We are well underway, with the assistance of leading outside experts and our own team, with efforts to further strengthen our defenses against future attacks.

III. Communication with Federal Law Enforcement and Government Authorities

We are grateful for the constructive relationship and cooperation of our federal regulators in our efforts to respond to the attack and get the pipeline restarted as quickly as possible.

On the morning of the attack, we proactively reached out to the Federal Bureau of Investigation (FBI) to inform them that cyber criminals had attacked Colonial Pipeline. We also scheduled a call within hours to debrief both the

FBI and the Cybersecurity & Infrastructure Security Agency (CISA) with information about the attack, and we remained in regular communication with law enforcement. We proactively shared Indicators of Compromise (IOCs) with law enforcement as well as other valuable threat intelligence in an effort to help thwart these kinds of attacks in the future, and assist the federal government with its endeavor to bring the criminals to justice.

We also have worked closely with the White House and National Security Council, the Department of Energy, which was designated as the lead Federal agency, as well as with the Department of Homeland Security, the Pipeline and Hazardous Materials Safety Administration (PHMSA), the Federal Energy Regulatory Commission (FERC), the Energy Information Administration, and the Environmental Protection Agency (EPA).

Our cooperation with federal agencies continues to this day, which is why I am grateful for your invitation to be here today and am pleased to support your efforts in determining how government can play a role in helping private companies better defend themselves against similar threats.

Our engagement with those federal authorities helped us achieve meaningful milestones in our response process to address the attack and restore pipeline operations as quickly as possible. In particular, we are appreciative for the cooperative way that federal agencies worked with us. Their focused collaboration made it easier to restart the pipelines and improved the speed with which we could transport fuels to their destinations.

IV. Post-Attack Response

We take our role in the United States infrastructure system very seriously. We recognize the gravity of the disruption that followed the shutdown, including panic-buying and shortages on the East Coast, and we express our sincerest regret to everyone who was impacted by this attack. The interests of our customers, shippers and the country are our top priorities and have been guiding our response.

I want to emphasize that the importance of protecting critical infrastructure drove the decision to halt operations of the pipeline to help ensure that the malware was not able to spread to our OT network. When we learned of the attack, we did not know the point of origination of the attack nor the scope of it, so bringing the entire system down was the surest way— and the right way—to contain any potential damage.

After halting operations, we took steps to continue to move product manually where we could, while working systematically and methodically to scan all of our systems for any potential malware or indicators of compromise.

Once we knew we could safely restart the pipeline, we worked as quickly as possible to get our pipeline back up and running. Bringing our pipeline back online is not as easy as "flicking a switch on," as President Biden correctly stated. It is an extraordinarily intricate and complex system, and this process required diligence and a herculean, around-the-clock effort to restore our full OT network and begin returning all pipelines to service on Wednesday evening, May 12.

While working through the restart process, we increased air surveillance, drove over 29,000 miles while inspecting our pipeline, and worked with local law enforcement agencies to secure our physical pipeline. Employees manually collected and real-time reported key pipeline information along our entire system to ensure the integrity of the system while our OT was not visible. We worked tirelessly to restore system integrity and bring the pipeline back in service as soon as we could do so safely.

Being extorted by criminals is not a position any company wants to be in. As I have stated publicly, I made the decision that Colonial Pipeline would pay the ransom to have every tool available to us to swiftly get the pipeline back up and running. It was one of the toughest decisions I have had to make in my life. At the time, I kept this information close hold because we were concerned about operational security and minimizing publicity for the threat actor. But I believe that restoring critical infrastructure as quickly as possible, in this situation, was the right thing to do for the country. We took steps in advance of making the ransom payment to follow regulatory guidance and we have explained our course of dealings with the attackers to law enforcement so that they can pursue enforcement options that may be available to them.

V. Ongoing Investigation into How This Happened and What We Can Do to Further Strengthen Our Defenses

Colonial Pipeline is an accountable organization, and that starts with taking proactive steps to prevent an attack like this from happening again. To further strengthen our defenses against future threats and cybersecurity attacks, we need to get to the bottom of how this one occurred. Over the past four weeks, we have learned a great deal. But forensic investigations, as many of you know, take time. Our experts are reviewing massive amounts of evidence and indicators of compromise and devoting ample resources to retracing the attackers' footsteps so we know, if possible, exactly where they got in, how they were able to move within our systems and what they may have been able to access. That investigation is ongoing, and while we may not have all of the answers today to the questions that you have, we are working hard to get them.

Although the investigation is ongoing, we believe the attacker exploited a legacy virtual private network (VPN) profile that was not intended to be in use. We are still trying to determine how the attackers gained the needed credentials to exploit it.

We have worked with our third-party experts to resolve and remediate this issue; we have shut down the legacy VPN profile, and we have implemented additional layers of protection across our enterprise. We also recently engaged Dragos' Rob Lee, one of the world's leading industrial and critical infrastructure and OT security specialists to work alongside Mandiant and assist with the strengthening of our other cyber defenses. We have also retained John Strand from Black Hills Information Security, another leader in the cybersecurity space, who will provide additional support to strengthen our cybersecurity program.

It will take time to review all the evidence to make sure we get the most accurate answers possible, and we will continue to look for ways to further enhance our cybersecurity. We're committed to sharing lessons learned with the government and our industry peers. As painful as this experience has been for us and those that rely on our pipeline, it is also an opportunity to learn more about how these criminals operate so that we and others can better protect ourselves moving forward.

Once we complete our investigation into this event, we plan to partner with the government and law enforcement and share those learnings with our peers in the infrastructure space, and more broadly across other sectors, so that they too learn from this event.

VI. Federal Government Response Going Forward

I recognize that Congress and federal agencies have been discussing what additional regulations may be appropriate in the wake of this ransomware attack. As the leader of Colonial Pipeline, I have been focused on restoring our normal operations and further strengthening our cyber defenses. One recommendation I have is to designate a single point of contact to coordinate the federal response to these types of events. Having a single point of contact was helpful and constructive as Colonial Pipeline worked around the clock to respond to the ransomware attack and restore operations, and I believe that would be valuable in the event of future cyberattacks.

There are also limits to what any one company can do. Colonial Pipeline can—and we will—continue investing in cybersecurity and strengthening our systems. But criminal gangs and nation states are always evolving, sharpening their tactics, and working to find new ways to infiltrate the systems of

American companies and the American government. These attacks will continue to happen, and critical infrastructure will continue to be a target. Whichever organization may be designated as the single point of contact, Congress must ensure it is adequately staffed and resourced to support industry, facilitate information sharing, and respond appropriately. We will also need the continued support of law enforcement to disrupt cyber-crime networks and to bring attackers like DarkSide to justice.

VII. Conclusion

In closing, I want to reiterate that we were the victims of a ransomware attack by criminals. I am proud of the way we were able to react and respond. We quickly took measures to secure critical infrastructure, to notify the appropriate authorities, and to work to safely restore operations. I appreciate Congress' interest in this attack and the lessons it may have for government and industry, and I welcome the opportunity to answer your questions.

Post-Hearing Questions for the Record
Submitted to Joseph A. Blount, Jr.
From Senator Maggie Hassan

"Threats to Critical Infrastructure: Examining the Colonial Pipeline Cyber Attack"
June 8, 2021

1. Cybersecurity needs to be a team effort. Therefore, encouraging two-way information sharing and establishing effective private-public partnerships is really important. CISA can piece together a wider perspective on emerging cybersecurity threats when many individual companies share their individual, fragmented perspective. And companies can be proactive and alert when federal authorities better share threat information.

    a. What information do you believe needs to be shared, in each direction, to strengthen the public-private partnership needed to identify, mitigate, and prevent future cyberattacks?

    b. Given CISA's acknowledgement that it must protect any trade information it receives as part of an information sharing agreement, is there any good reason for not sharing information? What are the roadblocks?

Response: On the morning of the attack, we proactively contacted the Federal Bureau of Investigation (FBI) to inform them that cyber criminals had attacked Colonial Pipeline. We also scheduled another call within hours to brief both the FBI and the Cybersecurity & Infrastructure Security Agency (CISA) together with information about the attack, and we remained in regular communication with law enforcement. We proactively shared with law enforcement Indicators of Compromise (IOCs) and other threat intelligence in an effort to help thwart these kinds of attacks in the future and to assist the federal government. Additionally, given the sensitive nature of this information, maintaining the confidentiality of this data was vital.

As difficult as this experience has been for us and those that rely on our pipeline, it is also an opportunity to learn more about how these criminals operate so we and others can better protect ourselves moving forward. We are continuing to undertake a thorough forensic investigation into the attack and it will take time to review the evidence to make sure we get accurate answers. However, we have begun the process of sharing preliminary lessons learned with industry partners and peers, so that they too learn from this event. We look forward to continued engagement with CISA and other government entities as we work to share information in an effort to prevent attacks like this in the future. Of course given the nature of this information, maintaining the confidentiality of certain sensitive data and findings is vital to the future security of the pipeline.

2. There are a lot of federal agencies potentially involved with pipeline security.
   a. Prior to the attack, which federal agencies did Colonial usually interact with regarding cybersecurity issues?
   b. Was it usually the agencies who reached out to you, or did Colonial Pipeline proactively reach out to the agencies?
   c. In your view, how well did those interactions help you identify weaknesses and improve your cybersecurity?

Response: We are grateful for the constructive relationship and cooperation of our federal regulators both before and since the attack. In addition to our engagement with federal law enforcement authorities regarding the attack, as described in our response to Question 1, we have also worked closely with CISA, the White House and National Security Council, the Department of Energy, which was designated as the lead federal agency, as well as with the Department of Homeland Security, the Pipeline and Hazardous Materials Safety Administration (PHMSA), and the Federal Energy Regulatory Commission (FERC). Our engagement with those federal authorities, preexisting productive relationships, and history of contact in both directions helped us achieve meaningful milestones in our response process to address the attack and restore pipeline operations quickly and safely. In particular, we appreciate the cooperation of the federal agencies that worked with us in connection with the attack. Their focused collaboration facilitated our ability to restart the pipeline, so we could transport various types of fuel to their destinations.

Post-Hearing Questions for the Record
Submitted to Joseph Blount
From Senator Kyrsten Sinema

"Threats to Critical Infrastructure: Examining the Colonial Pipeline Cyber Attack"
June 8, 2021

1) Prior to the early May attack on Colonial Pipelines, what steps did your company take to prioritize cybersecurity? In retrospect, are there additional steps you could have taken to better prepare for an attack?
   a. **Response:** Colonial Pipeline takes cybersecurity and the integrity of our pipeline extremely seriously. Over the past few years, we have increased our level of spending on information technology (IT) over 50%. Additionally, our IT team has nearly doubled in size as we continue to make significant investments in seasoned technical talent, our infrastructure, industry partnerships, and technology to further harden our systems and strengthen our defenses. We are continually preparing for a range of cyber risks and we remain focused on enhancing our cybersecurity program by leveraging industry-leading vendors that have helped us take steps to further strengthen our cyber defenses going forward.

2) Aside from the Transportation Security Agency's May 27th Security Directive for critical pipeline operators, what additional steps does Colonial plan to take as a result of the attack? And what additional recommendations do you have for the federal government in responding to these types of attacks?
   a. **Response:** See Response to Question 1. Additionally, we are grateful for the immediate and sustained support of federal law enforcement and governmental authorities, including the White House. We proactively contacted federal authorities within hours of the attack and found them to be extremely helpful as we worked to quickly and safely restore and secure our operations. Two key takeaways from our experience were that it was critical to have a single point of contact with the federal government to ensure a swift and coordinated response, and that the coordinating entity prioritize preserving the confidentiality of sensitive data regarding the attack and the company's security infrastructure. The inter-agency approach implemented by the Biden Administration streamlined the federal government's response and was very valuable, but having a single point of contact enhanced our coordination efforts. Whichever organization may be designated as the single point of contact, Congress must ensure it is adequately staffed and resourced to support the industry, facilitate information sharing and the preservation of confidential information, and respond appropriately. It is also important that victims receive the continued support of law enforcement to disrupt cyber-crime networks and bring attackers like DarkSide to justice.

3) Throughout our country, we are increasingly reliant on interconnected devices and networks that help manage critical areas such as pipelines, healthcare, and energy. How does your company plan to address such concentrated cyber risks in your operations moving forward?
   a. **Response:** See Response to Question 1. In addition, Colonial retained some of the best experts in the industry to advise on further strengthening its defenses.

4) Shortly after the attack on Colonial Pipelines, JBS Foods, the world's largest meat processing company with a facility located in Arizona, became the victim of a similar ransomware attack. What lessons would you share with other business owners, such as JBS's incident response team, which will help them to overcome a major cyber incident?
   a. **Response:** As difficult as this experience has been for us and those that rely on our pipeline, it is also an opportunity to learn more about how these criminals operate so we and others can better protect ourselves moving forward. We are continuing to undertake a thorough forensic investigation into the attack and it will take time to review the evidence to make sure we get accurate answers. We have already begun the process of sharing preliminary lessons learned with industry partners and peers, so that they too learn from this event.

5) Given that many cyber incidents start with poor cybersecurity practices by just one person inside an organization, does the entire staff of Colonial Pipelines receive cyber hygiene training? If so, can you generally describe the training they receive?
   a. **Response:** We leverage a number of industry-leading vendors that have helped us take steps to strengthen our cyber defenses over the past few years and provide redundant controls and enhanced capabilities. Some of the implemented measures specific to employee training include requiring mandatory annual physical and cybersecurity training as well as conducting simulated cyberattacks. Colonial provides training for employees at least annually on cybersecurity risks and engages employees through Cybersecurity Awareness Month.

Post-Hearing Questions for the Record
Submitted to Joseph A. Blount, Jr.
From Ranking Member Rob Portman

"Threats to Critical Infrastructure: Examining the Colonial Pipeline Cyberattack"
June 8, 2021

1. What Colonial employees or agents acting on behalf of Colonial communicated with DarkSide regarding the ransom payment?
    a. **Response:** Colonial did not communicate directly with the attackers. Rather, the communication with the attackers was handled by external negotiators, who were retained for this purpose.

2. What was DarkSide's initial ransom demand?
    a. **Response:** DarkSide's initial ransom demand that appeared on the initial notice of the attack was for "$4.8 million now or $9.6 million after doubled."

3. Did Colonial employees or any entity acting on behalf of Colonial inform the U.S. Government of their intent to pay the ransom prior to making the payment? Please specifically indicate whether Colonial employees or anyone acting on its behalf informed FBI, OFAC, or other government entity. If so, what advice or information did that entity provide in response?
    a. **Response:** Colonial called the FBI the morning of May 7, 2021, which is the day we became aware of the ransomware attack. We also had a call with the FBI and CISA together several hours later. On those calls, we did not indicate our intent to pay the ransom as we had not determined whether to do so at that time. We were aware of the FBI, OFAC, and other government entities' positions on ransom payments and our external experts checked OFAC's sanctions list to ensure that DarkSide was not on the list before we decided to pay the ransom. Additionally, during the May 7, 2021 telephone call we conducted with CISA and the FBI, the FBI indicated that the attackers were not sanctioned actors.

4. Please describe any sanctions compliance due diligence undertaken by Colonial or agents acting on behalf of Colonial prior to making the ransom payment.
    a. **Response:** See Response to Question 3.

5. Who purchased and transferred the 75 Bitcoin ransom to DarkSide? Please include the titles of any Colonial officers or senior employees and the names of any other organizations involved and their roles.
    a. **Response:** Payment was handled by third-party negotiators.

6. What steps, if any, did Colonial take while paying the ransom to facilitate the FBI's partial recovery of the ransom?
    a. **Response:** Beginning on the morning of the attack, we quickly provided the FBI with extensive information about the attack and perpetrator, including the bitcoin wallet on Saturday afternoon. We continued to cooperate and provide relevant information. We understand that this cooperation aided law enforcement in the recovery of the ransom payment.

7. Once DarkSide compromised Colonial's networks, did the attackers demonstrate a particular interest in specific sensitive information held by the company? If so, what specific sensitive information was targeted?
    a. **Response:** Our forensic investigation is ongoing and our experts continue to review the files that were exfiltrated. Based on the findings to date, we have no reason to believe that the attackers had a particular interest in specific sensitive information held by the company.
8. What sensitive information was exfiltrated by DarkSide in its attack?
    a. **Response:** Our forensic investigation is ongoing and our experts continue to review the files that were exfiltrated.
9. How did the exfiltration of this information contribute to Colonial's decision to pay the ransom?
    a. **Response:** Colonial Pipeline CEO Joe Blount stated publicly that this was one of the toughest decisions he ever had to make. Colonial's focus was to safely secure and restart the pipeline as quickly as possible. We believe this was the right thing to do for the country and our shippers.
10. During the hearing, Mr. Blount indicated Colonial had good backups. How long did it take for Colonial to bring these backups online?
    a. **Response:** We are proud and grateful to report that our response worked: we were able to quickly identify, isolate, and respond to the attack and stop the malware from spreading and causing even more damage. We then turned to remediating the problem and safely restoring service, and our backups were critical in achieving that quickly. The backups allowed us to begin to bring our critical systems back online within hours of containment and restore functionality. The containment and restoration took several days to complete, and we took steps to make all tools available to complete this process safely and efficiently. We are well underway, with the assistance of leading outside experts and our own team, with efforts to further strengthen our defenses against future attacks.

**Post-Hearing Questions for the Record
Submitted to Joseph A. Blount, Jr.
From Senator Josh Hawley**

**"Threats to Critical Infrastructure: Examining the Colonial Pipeline Cyber Attack"
June 8, 2021**

1. In the recent hearing on the Colonial Pipeline cyber-attack, you testified that your company invested approximately $200 million over the past five years in its IT system. Of that total, you did not know how much was specifically invested in cybersecurity. In addition, public reporting has suggested that in 2018, your company paid nearly $670 million to its owners in the form of dividends. Given this, please clarify the following:

    a. Of the $200 million that Colonial Pipeline invested in its IT system over five years, how much of that total was spent on cybersecurity?
    b. In 2016, how much did Colonial Pipeline invest in cybersecurity? And how much did Colonial Pipeline pay its owners in dividends?

c. In 2017, how much did Colonial Pipeline invest in cybersecurity? And how much did Colonial Pipeline pay its owners in dividends?
d. In 2018, how much did Colonial Pipeline invest in cybersecurity? And how much did Colonial Pipeline pay its owners in dividends?
e. In 2019, how much did Colonial Pipeline invest in cybersecurity? And how much did Colonial Pipeline pay its owners in dividends?
f. In 2020, how much did Colonial Pipeline invest in cybersecurity? And how much did Colonial Pipeline pay its owners in dividends?

Response: Colonial Pipeline takes cybersecurity and the integrity of our pipeline extremely seriously. Over the past five years, we have spent more than $200 million on our information technology ("IT") systems, including on multi-year improvements. The investments we have made in hardening and improving our IT systems are inextricably linked to the maintenance and performance of our systems and therefore are a critical part of our cybersecurity efforts. In addition, the benefits of our IT investments extend beyond the year when the improvement was made. Increased investment in IT has been and continues to be a priority for Colonial. Over the past few years, we have increased total spending on our IT program by more than 50 percent. Additionally, our IT team has nearly doubled in size. As part of our post-incident plan going forward, we will be assessing whether and where we may make further investments.

Information on dividend payments made by Colonial Pipeline Company for all requested years is available in the "Statement of Cash Flows" section on Colonial Pipeline Company's Form 6, which is filed on the FERC website at https://www.ferc.gov/industries-data/oil/general-information/oil-industry-forms/form-66-q-data-current-and-historical.

Chapter 2

Pipeline Cybersecurity: Federal Programs*

**Paul W. Parfomak
and Chris Jaikaran**

Summary

The vast U.S. network of natural gas, crude oil, and refined product pipelines is integral to U.S. energy supply and also has vital links to other critical infrastructure such as power plants and airports. This network is vulnerable to cyberattacks. Pipeline companies employ technologies which enable them to achieve business and operational efficiencies, but these technologies are susceptible to cybersecurity risks—and these risks have been growing. The May 2021 ransomware attack against the Colonial Pipeline, which disrupted gasoline supplies throughout the East Coast, highlighted this risk and increased concern in Congress about federal oversight of pipeline cybersecurity. Several bills in the 117th Congress would affect federal pipeline cybersecurity programs, including the Pipeline Security Act (H.R. 3243), the Pipeline and LNG Facility Cybersecurity Preparedness Act (H.R. 3078), and the Promoting Interagency Coordination for Review of Natural Gas Pipelines Act (H.R. 1616). In addition, the Colonial Pipeline incident has led to changes in the federal agency oversight of pipeline cybersecurity under existing statutory authorities.

Pipelines face varied cybersecurity risks. Pipelines rely on information technology (IT), such as laptops, and operational technology (OT), such as pipeline control systems. Using both types of systems creates challenges for cybersecurity. Attacks against IT can compromise the data and business systems of a company. Attacks against OT can

---

* This is an edited, reformatted and augmented version of Congressional Research Service Publication No. R46903, dated September 9, 2021.

In: Infrastructure Cybersecurity
Editor: Michael V. Walls
ISBN: 979-8-89113-039-5
© 2023 Nova Science Publishers, Inc.

cause physical disruptions that increase the probability of pipeline failure and environmental damage. Some attacks to IT (e.g., ransomware) can have an effect on OT as well, if they spread to those systems or the company opts to shut down its OT to prevent further damage.

Two agencies within the Department of Homeland Security have primary responsibility for pipeline cybersecurity: the Transportation Security Administration (TSA) and the Cybersecurity and Infrastructure Security Agency (CISA). TSA has had regulatory authority for security over all transportation—including pipelines—for two decades. For most of this time, TSA relied on voluntary pipeline cybersecurity guidance and best practices. The agency recently imposed mandatory requirements for pipeline cybersecurity after the Colonial Pipeline attack, when it issued two cybersecurity directives. CISA has more extensive cybersecurity capabilities and provides technical expertise to assist both TSA and industry partners in improving cybersecurity. CISA has conducted cyber risk assessments of pipeline operators and has received cybersecurity incident reports from companies pursuant to TSA's pipeline cybersecurity directives. Other federal entities also are involved with pipeline cybersecurity. They include the Department of Transportation's Pipeline and Hazardous Materials Safety Administration, which is the nation's pipeline safety regulator and partners with TSA on security issues, and the Department of Energy's (DOE's) Cybersecurity, Energy Security, and Emergency Response office, which is congressionally mandated to research cybersecurity risks and coordinate federal response to energy sector cyber incidents.

The Government Accountability Office, federal agencies, and industry stakeholders have raised several specific pipeline cybersecurity issues of ongoing interest to Congress. They include the following:

- *Resources.* TSA resources devoted to pipelines (and cybersecurity thereof) have been small relative to its other priorities (e.g., aviation). TSA officials have testified that the agency will increase staffing in fiscal years 2021 and 2022, but it is uncertain whether the increases will be sufficient to manage cyber risk.
- *Standards.* With the issuance of TSA's directives, questions around cybersecurity standards have arisen. TSA is requiring process standards (e.g., having a process to report incidents) rather than design standards (e.g., prescribing a technical specification for user access controls). The sufficiency of this approach is under debate.
- *Agency Roles. Whether* other federal agencies should have responsibility for pipeline cybersecurity has been under discussion. For example, some have argued for DOE to expand further into pipeline cybersecurity or for the Federal Energy Regulatory Commission to regulate pipeline operators.

- *Threat Information.* The quality, quantity, and timeliness of cybersecurity risk information originating with the government and being shared with the private sector continues to be an area of focus.

In addition to these specific issues, Congress may want to assess how the various elements of U.S. pipeline cybersecurity and critical infrastructure security will fit together most effectively in the nation's overall strategy to protect critical pipelines.

Pipeline security necessarily involves various groups: federal agencies, pipeline associations, large and small pipeline operators, and the broader industrial cybersecurity community. Reviewing how these groups work together to achieve common goals could be an overarching challenge for Congress.

Introduction

Pipeline The U.S. energy pipeline network is composed of approximately 3 million miles of pipeline transporting natural gas, crude oil, refined products, and other hazardous liquids.[1] This vast pipeline network is vital to the economy and integral to the nation's energy supply, with links to power plants, refineries, airports, and other critical infrastructure. Although pipelines are regarded as a relatively safe means of transporting materials, they have the potential to cause public injury and environmental harm. Both because of their economic importance and the physical risks they may pose, pipeline systems have drawn attention as targets for terrorism or other malicious activity. Physical attacks on pipelines were historically a priority, but the sophisticated computer systems used to administer and operate pipelines increasingly have become a target of cyberattacks. The May 8, 2021, ransomware attack on the Colonial Pipeline Company, which disrupted gasoline supplies throughout the East Coast, was the most significant attack on a U.S. pipeline computer system. However, pipeline cyberattacks have been occurring for at least a decade.

The Colonial Pipeline incident and previous pipeline cyberattacks have elevated concern in Congress about the cybersecurity of the nation's energy pipelines and federal programs to protect them. A July 13, 2021, report from the House Committee on Homeland Security stated, "as illustrated by the May

---

[1] Pipeline and Hazardous Materials Safety Administration (PHMSA), "Annual Report Mileage Summary Statistics," online tables, May 3, 2021, https://www.phmsa.dot.gov/ data-and-statistics/pipeline/annual-report-mileage-summary- statistics.

2021 Colonial Pipeline attack, the need for the Federal government to raise the bar on cybersecurity among pipeline operators is particularly acute."[2] Several bills in the 117th Congress would affect federal pipeline cybersecurity programs, including the Pipeline Security Act (H.R. 3243), the Pipeline and LNG Facility Cybersecurity Preparedness Act (H.R. 3078), and the Promoting Interagency Coordination for Review of Natural Gas Pipelines Act (H.R. 1616). In addition, the Colonial Pipeline incident has already led to significant changes in the federal oversight of pipeline cybersecurity under existing statutory authorities.

This report discusses cybersecurity risks to natural gas, oil, and refined products pipelines, including to control systems and information technology, as well as ransomware. It summarizes the history of major pipeline cybersecurity warnings and cyberattacks in the United States over the last 15 years. It examines the federal role in protecting U.S. pipelines from cyber threats, including the agencies involved and their pipeline cybersecurity activities. It discusses the federal response to the Colonial Pipeline cyberattack. The report concludes with an overview of selected issues for Congress, including legislative proposals to change federal pipeline security programs.

Cybersecurity Risks

Pipeline companies simultaneously operate two different types of technology systems— information technology (IT) and operational technology (OT). Both types of systems create challenges for cybersecurity. IT systems are common across many consumer and business products. IT includes the laptops, software, and networking equipment used for productivity and communications. OT enables cyber-physical linkages which allow dispersed equipment to be centrally monitored and controlled. OT includes industrial control systems (ICS) such as supervisory control and data acquisition (SCADA) systems, distributed control systems, and programmable logic controllers. IT and OT both may be enabled by Internet of Things (IoT) devices, such as a smart card reader to unlock a door, or a thermometer to maintain proper temperature at a fuel processing facility. IT and OT systems also may share connections, such as an OT system that reports usage (e.g.,

---

[2] U.S. Congress, House Homeland Security Committee, *Pipeline Security Act*, 117th Cong., 1st sess., July 13, 2021, H.Rept. 117-85, p. 3.

pipeline shipments) to an IT system that facilitates customer scheduling and billing. The complexity of simultaneously operating both types of systems can create novel opportunities for malicious actors to gain access and manipulate systems.

Industrial Control Systems (ICS) Risks

ICS are a type of OT used to monitor and control many aspects of network operation for railways, power grids, water and sewer systems—and pipeline networks. One category of ICS widely used in pipelines networks—SCADA systems—collects data (e.g., line pressure) in real time from sensors throughout a network and displays those data to human operators in remote network control rooms. These operators can then send computerized commands from SCADA workstations to control geographically dispersed equipment such as pipeline valves, pumps, meters, and many other network components. The SCADA system provides continuous feedback about conditions throughout the pipeline network and generates safety alarms when operating conditions fall outside prescribed levels.[3] ICS communications may employ dedicated telephone landlines, wireless communications (satellite, microwave, and radio), cellular telephone service, Wi-Fi, and the internet. As SCADA technology has matured, system control has become more intelligent and more automated, requiring less human intervention.

Historically, pipeline SCADA systems employed highly customized proprietary software and were physically isolated from external communications and computer networks. Because many of these systems were largely unique to a specific system operator, malicious actors outside the company faced challenges when trying to access and disrupt a SCADA system. But these unique systems were expensive to design, build, and maintain. Due to advancements in computer technology and the development and adoption of advanced communications and internet-based control system applications, SCADA systems have become more standardized and vulnerable to outside intrusion and manipulation.[4] Specific SCADA security weaknesses

---

[3] National Transportation Safety Board, Supervisory Control and Data Acquisition (SCADA) in Liquid Pipelines, NTSB/SS-05/02, November 29, 2005, pp. 1-2.
[4] Tobias Walk, "Cyber-Attack Protection for Pipeline SCADA Systems," Pipelines International Digest, January 2012, p. 6; Rose Tsang, Cyberthreats, "Vulnerabilities and Attacks on SCADA Networks," working paper, University of California, Goldman School of Public Policy, 2009, p. 2, http://gspp.berkeley.edu/iths/Tsang_SCADA%20Attacks.pdf.

include the adoption of standardized control system technologies (some with known vulnerabilities), increased connection to external networks, insecure communication connections, and the public availability of sensitive information about control systems and infrastructure.[5]

Once accessible to a knowledgeable attacker, a SCADA system can be exploited in a number of specific ways to carry out a cyberattack:

- issuing unauthorized commands to control equipment;
- sending false information to a control-system operator to initiate inappropriate action;
- disrupting control system operation by delaying or blocking the flow of information through the control network;
- making unauthorized changes to control system software to modify alarm thresholds or other configuration settings; and
- rendering resources unavailable by propagating malicious software (e.g., a virus, worm, Trojan horse) through the control network.[6]

In 2014, the Department of Homeland Security (DHS) released information on a project which demonstrated these vulnerabilities.[7] "Project Aurora" was conducted in 2007 by Idaho National Laboratory as a proof-of-concept cyberattack with physical consequences. In this attack, researchers exploited a system vulnerability to gain access to the ICS of a power generator. They proceeded to send commands to the generator to rapidly increase its revolutions, then quickly reverse them, and then repeat that cycle. Concurrently, researchers directed the ICS system to report to the monitoring system that the generator was operating normally. Video of the experiment shows the generator struggle under the malicious command sequence and ultimately fail.

Depending upon the configuration of a particular pipeline system, cyberattacks on ICS potentially could disrupt service, damage equipment, or even cause a hazardous release of pipeline contents. While no pipeline releases

---

[5] General Accounting Office, Critical Infrastructure Protection: Challenges and Efforts to Secure Control Systems, GAO-04-354, 2004, pp. 12-13; Eric Byres, "Next Generation Cyberattacks Target Oil and Gas SCADA," Pipeline & Gas Journal, February 2012; Robert O'Harrow Jr., "Cyber Search Engine Exposes Vulnerabilities," Washington Post, June 3, 2012. The General Accounting Office subsequently was renamed the Government Accountability Office.
[6] Tobias Walk, 2012, pp. 7-8.
[7] "The Aurora Project: An Epiphany on Hacking," SecureTheGrid, at https://securethegrid.com/destruction-by- cyberattack/.

due to a cyberattack have been reported publicly in the United States, such an attack reportedly was used in 2008 to cause an explosion of the Baku-Tbilisi-Ceyhan oil pipeline in Turkey.[8]

Information Technology Risks and Ransomware

Ransomware is a particular form of malicious software (malware) which seeks to deny users access to data and IT systems by encrypting the files and systems—thus locking out users. Perpetrators usually extort victims for payment, typically in cryptocurrency, to decrypt the system. Recently, such attacks have been coupled with data breaches in which perpetrators also steal data from their ransomware victims. In addition to locking their computer systems, the perpetrators notify victims that they have copies of their data and will release sensitive information unless a ransom is paid, extorting them twice. Colonial Pipeline fell victim to the DarkSide ransomware-as-a-service (RaaS) variant. RaaS is a cybercrime model in which one criminal group develops the ransomware and hosts the infrastructure upon which it operates, then leases that capability to another criminal group to conduct an attack.

Pipeline OT operators are exposed to ransomware risks (as are many other industries) to the extent that they have internet-connected IT. In the case of Colonial Pipeline, it was the IT which experienced the ransomware attack. To prevent further potential spread of the attack from the IT systems to their OT systems through some possible (but unknown) pathway, the pipeline operators chose temporarily to disconnect their IT from their OT. Doing so effectively shut down their entire pipeline system.

Pipeline Cybersecurity Warnings and Incidents

Federal security officials and industry analysts have long identified pipelines in the United States as potential targets for intentional disruption, although the degree of cyber risk has been steadily growing.[9] For example, a 2011 DHS pipeline threat assessment concluded that "terrorist groups have discussed

---

[8] Jordan Robertson and Michael Riley, "Mysterious '08 Turkey Pipeline Blast Opened New Cyberwar," Bloomberg, December 10, 2014.
[9] "Already Hard at Work on Security, Pipelines Told of Terrorist Threat," Inside FERC, McGraw-Hill Companies, January 3, 2002; Jennifer Alvey, "Cybersecurity: A 'Virtual' Reality," Public Utilities Fortnightly, September 15, 2003.

attacks on unspecified SCADA systems, but it is uncertain whether al-Qa'ida or any other group has the capability to conduct a successful cyberattack on these systems."[10] In 2016, the President of the Association of Oil Pipe Lines testified that cybersecurity threats to pipelines were increasing and that "there is a great concern about ... being prepared for cyberattacks."[11] A 2018 Government Accountability Office (GAO) study stated that "new threats to the nation's pipeline systems have evolved to include ... cyberattack or intrusion by nations."[12] In 2019, the President of the Interstate Natural Gas Association of America similarly stated,

> Threats are evolving. Not very long ago, the biggest threats to pipeline operators were the threat of physical damage from a third-party excavator and the threat of financial data compromise from cyber criminals. We now are concerned with the threat from sophisticated, well-resourced nation state actors. These threat actors are motivated and have the technical means to develop zero-day malware that can go undetected in a system for long periods.[13]

Also in 2019, the then-Director of National Intelligence singled out pipelines as critical infrastructure vulnerable to cyberattacks that could cause shutdowns "for days to weeks."[14] On June 6, 2021, the Secretary of Energy stated in an interview, "even as we speak, there are thousands of [cyber]attacks on all aspects of the energy sector."[15]

Growing warnings about pipeline cybersecurity threats have paralleled public reports about significant cyberattacks on U.S. pipelines.

---

[10] Transportation Security Administration, Office of Intelligence, Pipeline Threat Assessment, January 18, 2011, p. 3.

[11] Andrew Black, President and CEO, Association of Oil Pipe Lines, testimony before the House Committee on Homeland Security, Transportation and Protective Security Subcommittee hearing on "Pipelines: Securing the Veins of the American Economy," April 19, 2016.

[12] Government Accountability Office (GAO), Critical Infrastructure Protection: Actions Needed to Address Significant Weaknesses in TSA's Pipeline Security Program Management, GAO-19-48, December 2018, p. 1.

[13] Donald Santa, Interstate Natural Gas Association of America, Remarks at the Federal Energy Regulatory Commission Security Investments for Infrastructure Technical Conference, March 28, 2019, https://www.ingaa.org/ File.aspx?id=36642&v=62328155. Zero-day malware is malware which is newly discovered or takes advantage of previously unknown vulnerabilities.

[14] Daniel R. Coats, Director of National Intelligence, Worldwide Threat Assessment of the U.S. Intelligence Community, January 29, 2019, Statement for the Record before the Senate Select Committee on Intelligence, January 29, 2019, p. 5.

[15] Jennifer Granholm, Secretary of Energy, Cable News Network (CNN), television interview, June 6, 2021.

- In March 2012, the Industrial Control Systems Cyber Emergency Response Team within DHS "positively identified" an ongoing series of cyber intrusions among U.S. natural gas pipeline operators dating back to December 2011 as "related to a single campaign."[16] In July 2021, the Cybersecurity and Infrastructure Security Agency and the Federal Bureau of Investigation jointly announced that this campaign had targeted 23 pipeline operators. The agencies attributed the attacks to Chinese state-sponsored actors seeking "to help China develop cyberattack capabilities against U.S. pipelines to physically damage pipelines or disrupt pipeline operations."[17]
- In June 2014, a global cybersecurity company reported "an ongoing cyberespionage campaign" by a group known as Dragonfly against "strategically important" U.S. and international targets, primarily in the energy sector, including petroleum pipeline operators.[18]
- In December 2016, the Department of Transportation's (DOT's) Pipeline and Hazardous Materials Safety Administration issued an Advisory Bulletin regarding cybersecurity threats to pipeline SCADA systems, stating that it was "aware of prior intrusion attempts on pipeline infrastructure."[19]
- In March 2018, the DHS Cybersecurity and Infrastructure Security Agency (CISA) issued a cybersecurity alert "on Russian government actions," which included targets in the U.S. energy sector.[20]
- In April 2018, several major U.S. natural gas pipeline companies reported IT cyberattacks on the third-party data interchange systems used to communicate with customers.[21]

---

[16] Industrial Control Systems Cyber Emergency Response Team (ICS-CERT), "Gas Pipeline Cyber Intrusion Campaign," ICS-CERT Monthly Monitor, April 2012, p. 1.
[17] Cybersecurity and Infrastructure Security Agency and Federal Bureau of Investigation, "Chinese Gas Pipeline Intrusion Campaign, 2011 to 2013," Joint Cybersecurity Advisory, Product ID: AA21-201A, July 20, 2021.
[18] A.L. Johnson, "Dragonfly: Western Energy Companies Under Sabotage Threat," Broadcom, cybersecurity blog, June 30, 2014, https://symantec-enterprise-blogs.security.com/blogs/threat-intelligence/dragonfly-energy-sector-cyber- attacks.
[19] PHMSA, "Pipeline Safety: Safeguarding and Securing Pipelines from Unauthorized Access," 81 Federal Register 89183, December 9, 2016.
[20] Cybersecurity and Infrastructure Security Agency (CISA), "Russian Government Cyber Activity Targeting Energy and Other Critical Infrastructure Sectors," Alert (TA18-074A), March 15, 2018.
[21] R. Collins, N. S. Malik, and M. Vamburkar, "Cyberattack Pings Data Systems of at Least Four Gas Networks," Bloomberg, April 4, 2018.

- In February 2020, CISA reported "a cyberattack affecting control and communication assets on the operational technology (OT) network of a natural gas compression facility," which led to a two-day pipeline shutdown. According to CISA, "the victim failed to implement robust segmentation between the IT and OT networks, which allowed the adversary to traverse the IT-OT boundary and disable assets on both networks."[22]
- On May 8, 2021, the Colonial Pipeline Company announced that it had halted its pipeline operations due to a ransomware attack, disrupting critical supplies of gasoline and other refined products throughout the East Coast for several days.[23] Although the attack targeted IT systems, the possibility that it could cross over to OT systems led to a precautionary shutdown.

In addition to these incidents, other significant pipeline cyberattacks may have occurred. However, they may not have been reported publicly for reasons including concern about company reputation, data privacy, or system security.

The Federal Role in Pipeline Cybersecurity

There are two federal agencies primarily responsible for pipeline cybersecurity—both part of DHS: the Transportation Security Administration (TSA) and the Cybersecurity and Infrastructure Security Agency (CISA). TSA has broad authorities for pipeline security (physical and cyber) and CISA has broad capabilities for managing cybersecurity risk across a variety of sectors and systems. In addition, other entities, both federal and nongovernmental, have roles in pipeline cybersecurity.

Transportation Security Administration

Federal pipeline security efforts originated in the pipeline safety program. The Natural Gas Pipeline Safety Act of 1968 (P.L. 90-481) and the Hazardous

---

[22] CISA, "Ransomware Impacting Pipeline Operations," Alert (AA20-049A), February 18, 2020.
[23] Colonial Pipeline, "Media Statement Update: Colonial Pipeline System Disruption," May 17, 2021, https://www.colpipe.com/news/press-releases/media-statement-colonial-pipeline-system-disruption.

Liquid Pipeline Act of 1979 (P.L. 96-129) are the principal early acts establishing the federal role in pipeline safety. Under both statutes, the Transportation Secretary is given primary authority to regulate key aspects of interstate pipeline safety: design, construction, operation and maintenance, and spill response planning. Presidential Decision Directive 63 (PDD-63), issued by President Bill Clinton in 1998, assigned to DOT the lead responsibility for pipeline security as well as safety.[24] In 2001, President George W. Bush signed the Aviation and Transportation Security Act (P.L. 107-71) establishing the Transportation Security Administration (TSA) within DOT. The act placed the DOT's pipeline security authority (under PDD-63) within TSA. The act specified a range of duties and powers related to general transportation security for TSA, including intelligence management, threat assessment, mitigation, and security measure oversight and enforcement.

In 2002, President George W. Bush signed the Homeland Security Act of 2002 (P.L. 107-296) creating DHS. Among other provisions, the act transferred TSA from DOT to DHS (§403). The Implementing Recommendations of the 9/11 Commission Act of 2007 (P.L. 110-53) directed TSA to promulgate pipeline security regulations and carry out necessary inspection and enforcement if the agency determines that regulations are appropriate (§1557(d)). Thus, TSA has primary responsibility and regulatory authority for the security of natural gas and hazardous liquid (e.g., oil, refined products, and carbon dioxide) pipelines in the United States. In 2018, TSA published its *Cybersecurity Roadmap* to guide the agency's "collective efforts to prioritize cybersecurity measures within TSA."[25] In addition to outlining TSA's own cybersecurity initiatives, the *Roadmap* states that TSA "will work with the Cybersecurity and Infrastructure Security Agency (CISA), with its mission to protect the critical infrastructure of the United States."[26]

Cybersecurity and Infrastructure Security Agency

Congress created CISA in the Cybersecurity and Infrastructure Security Agency Act of 2018 (P.L. 115-278); however, predecessor organizations executed similar authorities and capabilities.

---

[24] Presidential Decision Directive 63, Protecting the Nation's Critical Infrastructures, May 22, 1998.
[25] TSA, Cybersecurity Roadmap 2018, November 1, 2018.
[26] Ibid., p. 4.

Today, CISA's mission is to serve as "the Nation's risk advisor, working with partners to defend against today's threats and collaborating to build more secure and resilient infrastructure for the future."[27] CISA does this for cybersecurity and infrastructure security, and across the two security disciplines. CISA supports pipeline cybersecurity through its Integrated Operations Division and its National Risk Management Center. The Integrated Operations Division contains offices with the emergency response capabilities previously held and can conduct vulnerability assessments of ICS at the request of those systems' operators. The National Risk Management Center serves as CISA's planning, analysis, and collaboration center. Among other activities, the center piloted a pipeline cybersecurity initiative to identify and address cybersecurity risks to pipeline systems (discussed further under "TSA Collaboration with CISA").

On July 28, 2021, President Biden released the National Security Memorandum on *Improving Cybersecurity for Critical Infrastructure Control Systems*.[28] This memorandum directs the Secretaries of Homeland Security and Commerce (through CISA and the National Institute of Standards and Technology, NIST) to develop and issue performance goals for critical infrastructure owners and operators to follow regarding cybersecurity.

Other Pipeline Cybersecurity Organizations

In addition to TSA and CISA, three other entities play significant roles in pipeline cybersecurity, one federal and two nongovernmental: the Department of Energy's (DOE's) Cybersecurity, Energy Security, and Emergency Response (CESER) office, the Oil and Natural Gas Information Sharing and Analysis Center (ONG-ISAC), and the Downstream Natural Gas Information Sharing and Analysis Center (DNG-ISAC).

The Fixing America's Surface Transportation Act (FAST Act, P.L. 114-94) authorized DOE as the Sector-Specific Agency (i.e., the lead federal agency for security) for the energy sector.[29] The FAST Act also authorized

---

[27] CISA, "About CISA," June 20, 2021, https://www.cisa.gov/about-cisa.
[28] The White House, "Improving Cybersecurity for Critical Infrastructure Control Systems," National Security Memorandum, July 28, 2021, at https://www.whitehouse.gov/briefing-room/statements-releases/2021/07/28/national-security-memorandum-on-improving-cybersecurity-for-critical-infrastructure-control-systems/.
[29] Sector-Specific Agencies for critical infrastructure sectors were designated in Presidential Policy Directive-21, "Critical Infrastructure Security and Resilience," February 12, 2013.

DOE to establish and maintain a capability to manage cybersecurity risks to the energy sector, which DOE executes through CESER. The CESER office funds research and development, deploys monitoring tools to better understand evolving risks, conducts exercises, and coordinates federal responses to energy sector incidents (a role CESER played after the Colonial Pipeline cyberattack).

Pursuant to the Cybersecurity Act of 2015 (P.L. 114-113, Division N), ONG-ISAC and DNG- ISAC are recognized as information sharing and analysis organizations (ISAOs). As such, they can share among their sector membership information on cyber threats and measures to protect against those threats. Additionally, ISAC members can share this information with the government. The ONG-ISAC serves companies in oil and natural gas exploration and production, transportation, refining, and delivery. The DNG-ISAC serves natural gas distribution utilities and pipeline transmission companies. There is some overlap in membership across the two ISACs.

Federal Agency Pipeline Security Activities

TSA and CISA both have active programs in pipeline cybersecurity which encompass a range of related activities. In addition, other federal agencies, including DOT and DOE, support specific aspects of pipeline cybersecurity, either in cooperation with TSA and CISA or independently.

TSA Pipeline Security Program

TSA's pipeline security program currently is administered through the Surface Division in its Office of Security Operations.[30] Although TSA was given regulatory authority for pipeline security under P.L. 107-71 and P.L. 110-53, its activities prior to the Colonial Pipeline cyberattack relied upon voluntary industry compliance with the agency's security guidance and best practice recommendations.[31] In 2003, TSA initiated its ongoing pipeline Corporate Security Review Program, wherein the agency conducts voluntary visits with

---

[30] TSA, "TSA Organizational Chart," July 21, 2020, https://www.tsa.gov/sites/default/files/tsa_org_chart_matrix.pdf.
[31] Transportation Security Administration (TSA), Pipeline Security Guidelines, March 2018 (updated April 2021); and Pipeline Security Smart Practice Observations, September 19, 2011.

the largest pipeline and natural gas distribution operators "to assess the current security practices in the pipeline industry, with a focus on the physical and cybersecurity of pipelines" and the fuels they carry.[32] According to the agency, these reviews typically involve one to three TSA staff meeting with pipeline representatives at the operator's headquarters "to conduct a seven to eight hour interview" to "analyze the owner/operator's security plan and policies and compare their practices with recommendations in TSA's Pipeline Security Guidelines."[33]

P.L. 110-53 also specifically requires TSA to "develop and implement a plan for reviewing the pipeline security plans and an inspection of the critical facilities of the 100 most critical pipeline operators" (§1557(b)). To fulfill this mandate, in 2008 TSA initiated what is now the agency's Critical Facility Security Review Program, under which the agency conducts in-depth physical security reviews of all the critical facilities of the largest pipeline systems in the United States.[34] In this program, pipeline operators identify their own critical facilities based on the TSA Pipeline Security Guidelines. TSA visits these critical facilities and collects site-specific information from operators on facility security policies and procedures, and physical security measures.[35]

Since its formation, TSA has engaged in a number of other pipeline security initiatives, such as developing a statistical tool for risk ranking; publishing a security incident and recovery protocol plan; convening international pipeline security forums; developing pipeline security awareness training materials; convening periodic information-sharing conference calls and classified briefings about pipeline sector threats; and participating in pipeline sector coordinating groups.[36]

Pipeline cybersecurity has long been a distinct focus within TSA's overall pipeline security program. For example, in 2014, TSA was employing the Cybersecurity Assessment and Risk Management Approach in collaborating

---

[32] 84 Federal Register 128, July 3, 2019, p. 31896.
[33] Ibid.
[34] The current program originally was established as the Critical Facility Inspection Program. The program was renamed in FY2012 to reflect a change in the program from an inspection to a security review.
[35] 86 Federal Register 18291, April 8, 2021, pp. 18291-18292.
[36] Sonya T. Proctor, TSA, testimony before the House Committee on Homeland Security, Subcommittee on Transportation and Maritime Security and Subcommittee on Cybersecurity, Infrastructure Protection, and Innovation, hearing on "Cyber Threats in the Pipeline: Lessons from the Federal Response to the Colonial Pipeline Ransomware Attack," June 15, 2021; Jack Fox, TSA, Pipeline Security: An Overview of TSA Programs, slide presentation, May 5, 2014; TSA, Transportation Systems Sector-Specific Plan, 2010, p. 326.

with stakeholders to identify cyber risks to pipeline industry value chains, critical functions, and supporting cyber infrastructure.[37] TSA's current security guidelines include a dedicated section with cybersecurity provisions.[38] The TSA guidelines also state that pipeline operators "should consider the approach outlined" in the National Institute of Standards and Technology (NIST) *Framework for Improving Critical Infrastructure Cybersecurity*, other guidance issued by DHS and DOE, and "industry-specific or other established methodologies, standards, and best practices."[39]

TSA Collaboration with CISA

On October 3, 2018, DHS announced the Pipeline Cybersecurity Initiative, which "partners DHS cybersecurity resources, DOE's energy sector expertise, with TSA's regular and ongoing assessments of pipeline security to get a broader understanding of the risks the sector faces."[40] As part of this initiative, TSA began collaborating with CISA's Validated Architecture Design Reviews program in conducting voluntary cybersecurity assessments of pipeline operators. These reviews examine the alignment of pipeline IT or OT infrastructures with federal and industry standards, guidelines, and best practices for cybersecurity through a review of system information provided by pipeline operators and in-person (or virtual) interviews with operator staff.[41] TSA also has cooperated with the Federal Energy Regulatory Commission (FERC), which regulates bulk power system cybersecurity, in conducting voluntary joint Pipeline Cyber Architecture Reviews at select pipeline companies to assess "the pipeline system's cybersecurity

---

[37] Jack Fox, May 5, 2014.
[38] TSA, March 2018, Section 7.
[39] See National Institute of Standards and Technology, Framework for Improving Critical Infrastructure Cybersecurity, Version 1.1, April 16, 2018; and Department of Energy, Office of Cybersecurity, Energy Security, and Emergency Response, "Cybersecurity Capability Maturity Model (C2M2) Program," https://www.energy.gov/ceser/energy-security/cybersecurity-capability-maturity-model-c2m2-program, accessed June 9, 2021. Relevant industry standards include American Petroleum Institute (API), Pipeline SCADA Security (API Standard 1164, currently being updated); and the International Society of Automation and International Electrotechnical Commission (ISA/IEC) 62443 series of standards for industrial automation and control systems, among other standards.
[40] Department of Homeland Security (DHS), "DHS and DOE Meet with Oil and Natural Gas Sector Coordinating Council, Announce Pipeline Cybersecurity Initiative," press release, October 3, 2018.
[41] CISA, "Pipeline Cybersecurity Assessments Update," Oil and Natural Gas Subsector Coordinating Council / Energy Sector Government Coordinating Council Meeting, July 9, 2020, https://www.aga.org/globalassets/virtual-vadr-update-and-vadr_fact-sheet-new-2019.pdf.

environment of operational and business critical network controls."[42] CISA's Industrial Control Systems Joint Working Group, its National Cybersecurity and Communications Integration Center (NCCIC), and other multi-modal cybersecurity initiatives also involve pipeline operators.[43]

TSA Pipeline Cybersecurity Directives

On May 27, 2021, in response to the Colonial Pipeline cyberattack, TSA issued its first mandatory security requirements in the form of a Security Directive, applicable to owners and operators of critical pipeline facilities (as identified by TSA).[44] The directive requires that these companies designate and use a Cybersecurity Coordinator at the corporate level and report any cybersecurity incidents involving their systems to CISA within 12 hours. The directive also required pipeline companies to conduct a cybersecurity vulnerability assessment to determine whether their practices and systems align with TSA's pipeline security guidelines, identify gaps, identify remediation measures that will be taken to fill those gaps, and establish a timeline to implement those measures. Companies were required to report this information to TSA and CISA within 30 days.[45] According to TSA, 100% of companies subject to the directive did so.[46] The directive also states that company information submitted pursuant to the directive will be protected as Sensitive Security Information.[47] The directive is effective for one year but

---

[42] David P. Pekoske, TSA Administrator, letter to the Honorable Maria Cantwell, Senate Committee on Commerce, Science, and Transportation, March 21, 2019, https://www.eenews.net/assets/2019/06/27/document_ew_03.pdf; Sonya Proctor, Director, Surface Division, Policy, Plans, and Engagement, TSA, testimony before the House Committee on Homeland Security, Subcommittee on Transportation and Maritime Security, hearing on "Securing U.S. Surface Transportation from Cyberattacks," February 26, 2019.

[43] CISA, "Industrial Control Systems Joint Working Group (ICSJWG)," https://us-cert.cisa.gov/ics/Industrial-Control-Systems-Joint-Working-Group-ICSJWG; CISA, Securing Industrial Control Systems: A Unified Initiative, July 2020, p. 4. The NCCIC incorporates the functions of the former Industrial Control Systems Cyber Emergency Response Team (ICS-CERT).

[44] Under 49 U.S.C. §114(l)(2)(A), "if the [TSA] Administrator determines that a regulation or security directive must be issued immediately in order to protect transportation security, the Administrator shall issue the regulation or security directive without providing notice or an opportunity for comment and without prior approval of the Secretary."

[45] TSA, "Enhancing Pipeline Cybersecurity," Security Directive Pipeline-2021-01, May 27, 2021.

[46] David P. Pekoske, TSA Administrator, testimony before the Senate Committee on Commerce, Science, and Transportation, hearing on "Pipeline Cybersecurity: Protecting Critical Infrastructure," July 27, 2021.

[47] 49 C.F.R. §1520.

could be extended.[48] TSA's press release announcing the directive further stated that the agency was "also considering follow-on mandatory measures that will further support the pipeline industry in enhancing its cybersecurity."[49]

On June 15, 2021, the TSA Assistant Administrator, Surface Operations, testified that the agency was preparing a second directive with "more specific mitigation measures and ... requirements with regard to assessments," which would be "rather prescriptive in terms of the mitigation measures required." Compliance would be "subject to inspection" by transportation security inspectors who have received training in pipeline operations and cybersecurity from DOT's Pipeline and Hazardous Materials Safety Administration (PHMSA) and Idaho National Laboratory, respectively.[50]

On July 20, 2021, TSA announced its second pipeline cybersecurity directive, requiring critical pipeline owners and operators "to implement specific mitigation measures to protect against ransomware attacks and other known threats to information technology and operational technology systems, develop and implement a cybersecurity contingency and recovery plan, and conduct a cybersecurity architecture design review."[51] TSA's announcement did not provide more specific details because the specific security measures are considered Sensitive Security Information.[52] The TSA Administrator has stated that the NIST Cybersecurity Framework, which is referenced in the second directive, "would give an idea of some of the items that we require," and that the directive also mandates cyber architecture design reviews and contingency planning.[53] The TSA Administrator also has stated that the directive contains provisions whereby operators may seek approval for alternative procedures to any specific measures, providing flexibility for pipeline operators to achieve their intended security outcomes.[54] According to TSA's announcement, CISA advised the agency on pipeline cybersecurity threats and technical countermeasures during development of the directive.

---

[48] Under 49 U.S.C. §114(l)(2)(B), the duration of TSA's security directives may be extended indefinitely if ratified by the Transportation Security Oversight Board.

[49] TSA, "DHS Announces New Cybersecurity Requirements for Critical Pipeline Owners and Operators," press release, May 27, 2021.

[50] Sonya T. Proctor, June 15, 2021. Idaho National Laboratory runs the "Critical Infrastructure Protection Training" program. More information available at https://inl.gov/critical-infrastructure-protection-training/.

[51] Department of Homeland Security, "DHS Announces New Cybersecurity Requirements for Critical Pipeline Owners and Operators," press release, July 20, 2021.

[52] Sonya T. Proctor, June 15, 2021.

[53] David P. Pekoske, July 27, 2021.

[54] Ibid.

The second directive, like the first, is effective for one year, with the possibility of extension.

DHS and DOT Cooperation

In 2003, President George W. Bush issued Homeland Security Presidential Directive 7 (HSPD-7), clarifying executive agency responsibilities for identifying, prioritizing, and protecting critical infrastructure.[55] HSPD-7 required that DHS and DOT "collaborate in regulating the transportation of hazardous materials by all modes (including pipelines)." Pursuant to this directive, in 2004, the DHS and DOT entered into a memorandum of understanding (MOU) concerning their respective security roles in all modes of transportation. The MOU states that "specific tasks and areas of responsibility that are appropriate for cooperation will be documented in annexes ... individually approved and signed by appropriate representatives of DHS and DOT."[56] In 2006, the agencies signed an annex to the MOU, which was updated in 2020, "to delineate clear lines of authority and responsibility and promote communications, efficiency, and non-duplication of effort ... in the area of transportation security and safety."[57] In March 2010, TSA published a *Pipeline Security and Incident Recovery Protocol Plan* which details the separate and cooperative responsibilities of the two agencies with respect to a pipeline security incident.[58]

DHS and DOT have continued to cooperate on pipeline security in recent years. For example, TSA coordinated with PHMSA and other agencies to address ongoing vandalism and sabotage against critical pipelines by environmental activists in 2016.[59] In April 2016, the Director of TSA's Surface Division testified about the agency's relationship with DOT:

---

[55] HSPD-7 superseded PDD-63 (par. 37).
[56] Department of Homeland Security (DHS) and Department of Transportation (DOT), Memorandum of Understanding Between the Department of Homeland Security and the Department of Transportation on Roles and Responsibilities, September 28, 2004, p. 4.
[57] TSA and PHMSA, "Transportation Security Administration and Pipelines and Hazardous Materials Safety Administration Cooperation on Pipeline Transportation Security and Safety," February 26, 2020. This annex supersedes a prior version of the annex signed in 2006.
[58] TSA, Pipeline Security and Incident Recovery Protocol Plan, March 2010, p. 7.
[59] GAO, Critical Infrastructure Protection: Actions Needed to Address Significant Weaknesses in TSA's Pipeline Security Program Management, GAO-19-48, December 2018, p. 23.

Pipeline Cybersecurity

TSA and DOT co-chair the Pipeline Government Coordinating Council to facilitate information sharing and coordinate on activities including security assessments, training, and exercises. TSA and [PHMSA] work together to integrate pipeline safety and security priorities, as measures installed by pipeline owners and operators often benefit both safety and security.[60]

PHMSA issued a 2016 Advisory Bulletin on SCADA system security "in coordination with" TSA.[61] In July 2017, the two agencies collaborated on a web-based portal to facilitate sharing sensitive but unclassified incident information among federal agencies with pipeline responsibilities.[62] In February 2018, the Director of TSA's Surface Division again testified about cooperation with PHMSA, stating, "TSA works closely with [PHMSA] for incident response and monitoring of pipeline systems," although she did not provide specific examples.[63]

Following the Colonial Pipeline ransomware attack, PHMSA joined TSA and CISA on a teleconference call with pipeline operators to provide updates on the incident, answer questions, and provide resources to support cybersecurity mitigation efforts.[64] The Deputy Secretary of Transportation subsequently testified that PHMSA intends to "leverage its authorities to inspect and enforce three critical components of pipeline operations" related to cybersecurity: system control room regulations, integrity management plan requirements,[65] and emergency response plan regulations.[66] The Deputy Secretary also stated that DOT's Office of Intelligence, Security, and

---

[60] Sonya T. Proctor, Surface Division Director, TSA, testimony before the House Committee on Homeland Security, Subcommittee on Transportation Security hearing on "Pipelines: Securing the Veins of the American Economy," April 19, 2016.
[61] PHMSA, December 9, 2016.
[62] GAO, December 2018, p. 23.
[63] Sonya T. Proctor, TSA, testimony before the House Committee on Homeland Security Subcommittee on Transportation and Maritime Security and Subcommittee on Cybersecurity, Infrastructure Protection and Innovation, joint hearing on "Securing U.S. Surface Transportation from Cyberattacks," February 26, 2019.
[64] TSA, "TSA Response to Congressional Research Service Inquiry on Colonial Pipeline Incident," memorandum, June 29, 2021.
[65] "An integrity management program is a set of safety management, operations, maintenance, evaluation, and assessment processes that are implemented in an integrated and rigorous manner to ensure operators provide enhanced protection for [High-consequence Areas]." See PHMSA, "Overview: Integrity Management," https://primis.phmsa.dot.gov/comm/Im.htm.
[66] Polly Trottenberg, Deputy Secretary of Transportation, written testimony submitted for the Senate Committee on Commerce, Science, and Transportation, hearing on "Pipeline Cybersecurity: Protecting Critical Infrastructure," July 27, 2021, p. 3.

Emergency Response was collaborating with the National Security Council and interagency partners on a natural gas pipelines Industrial Control Systems Cybersecurity Initiative and that "DOT continues work with [its] sister agencies, especially TSA and CISA, to invest in world class research and pursue initiatives to address cybersecurity threats."[67]

DOE and National Laboratory Activities

DOE administers the Cybersecurity Capability Maturity Model (C2M2) Program, which "enables organizations to voluntarily measure the maturity of their cybersecurity capabilities in a consistent manner."[68] The program has published a sector-specific version of the C2M2 model tailored to the operations of the oil and natural gas industry, including pipelines.[69] DOE also operates the National SCADA Test Bed Program, a partnership with Idaho National Laboratory, Sandia National Laboratories, and other national laboratories to address control system security challenges in the energy sector. Among its key functions, the program performs control system testing, research, and development; control system requirements development; and industry outreach.[70] Sandia Laboratories also has performed authorized defensive cybersecurity assessments examining pipeline systems through its Information Design Assurance Red Team program.[71]

GAO Pipeline Security Reports

The TSA Modernization Act, part of the FAA Reauthorization Act of 2018 (P.L. 115-254, Division K, Title I, Subtitle G, §1980) mandated that GAO study the roles and responsibilities of DHS and DOT with respect to pipeline security. The act required examination of "strategic and operational

---

[67] Ibid., pp. 4-5.
[68] DOE, Office of Cybersecurity, Energy Security, and Emergency Response (CESER), "Cybersecurity Capability Maturity Model (C2M2) Program," https://www.energy.gov/ceser/energy-security/cybersecurity-capability-maturity- model-c2m2-program.
[69] DOE, "Cybersecurity Capability Maturity Model, Version 2.0," July 2021.
[70] DOE, Office of Electricity, "National SCADA Test Bed," https://www.energy.gov/oe/technology-development/energy-delivery-systems-cybersecurity/national-scada-test-bed.
[71] See, for example, Sandia National Laboratories, Information Design Assurance Red Team, "Addendum Report: Threat-Based Examination of NAESB Standards and Business Operations," July 15, 2019, https://www.naesb.org/pdf4/ bd_cic081419w1.pdf.

responsibilities for pipeline security" and other specific aspects of TSA's and industry's pipeline security activities (§1980(b)). In response to reporting requirements in the act, GAO published two separate reports, in 2018 and 2019.

GAO's first report, *Critical Infrastructure Protection: Actions Needed to Address Significant Weaknesses in TSA's Pipeline Security Program Management*, examined TSA's pipeline physical security and cybersecurity program.[72] The report was based upon an analysis of TSA documents, evaluation of TSA's pipeline risk assessments, and interviews with TSA officials, major U.S. pipeline operators, and pipeline industry trade association representatives. Among other findings, GAO's report identified several "weaknesses" in TSA's program management with specific relevance to pipeline cybersecurity.

- Pipeline operators interviewed by GAO reported using a range of guidelines and standards to address physical and cybersecurity risks. All had implemented TSA's voluntary guidelines, although the degree to which they had implemented them was not detailed in the report.
- Although TSA had revised its security guidelines to reflect dynamic threats and incorporate the NIST *Cybersecurity Framework*, the guidelines did not include all of the elements of the framework. TSA also lacked a documented process for regularly reviewing and revising its guidelines, so the agency could not ensure they reflected the latest standards and best practices.
- TSA guidelines lacked clear definitions of what constituted critical facilities, so a number of the largest pipeline system operators "deemed highest risk" had not identified any critical facilities.
- TSA had staffing variations in its pipeline security programs, with the number of full-time equivalent (FTE) employees over a nine-year period ranging between 14 FTEs (FY2012 and FY2013) and 1 FTE (FY2014). There were 6 FTEs in FY2018, the lowest staffing level reported.
- Pipeline operators and industry representatives reported that TSA lacked the expertise required to fully assess cybersecurity in security reviews. TSA did not, at the time, have a strategic workforce plan that identified staffing needs and skill sets such as cybersecurity.

---

[72] GAO, December 2018.

- TSA had not tracked the status of CSR recommendations among pipeline operators for over five years, and related security review data were not sufficiently reliable. Consequently, it was difficult for the agency to evaluate the performance of the pipeline security program.[73]

GAO made 10 recommendations to address the weaknesses it identified in TSA's program. TSA concurred with the recommendations and outlined specific steps it would take to address them. In addition, TSA stated that it would partner with CISA's National Risk Management Center "to conduct 10 in-depth cybersecurity reviews with pipeline companies during FY2019."[74] As of June 11, 2021, GAO reported that 3 of its 10 recommendations remained outstanding, including its recommendation that TSA "develop a strategic workforce plan ... which could include determining the number of personnel necessary to meet the goals set for its Pipeline Security Branch, as well as the knowledge, skills, and abilities, including cybersecurity."[75] TSA completed the Final Workforce Assessment Report in May 2021.[76] The report acknowledged that TSA lacks the qualified personnel with cybersecurity expertise to fully execute TSA's missions.

GAO's second report, Critical Infrastructure Protection: Key Pipeline Security Documents Need to Reflect Current Operating Environment, focused on the roles and responsibilities of DHS and DOT in pipeline security.[77] GAO concluded that, while the 2006 TSA-PHMSA MOU Annex delineated the agencies' mutually agreed-upon roles and responsibilities, it had not been reviewed to consider pipeline security developments since its inception. TSA's Pipeline Security and Incident Recovery Protocol Plan likewise had not been updated since it was issued in 2010 "to reflect changes in pipeline security threats, technology, federal law and policy, and any other factors."[78] Among other things, GAO recommended that TSA and PHMSA update these documents and put in place formal processes to periodically update them in the future. As noted above, TSA and PHMSA signed an update to the MOU

---

[73] GAO, December 2018, pp. 28-29, 32, 34, 38-40, 60.
[74] Ibid., p. 80.
[75] Ibid., p. 62.
[76] U.S. Government Accountability Office, Critical Infrastructure Protection: TSA is Taking Steps to Address Some Security Program Weaknesses, GAO-21-105263, July 27, 2021, pp. 12-13, https://www.gao.gov/assets/gao-21- 105263.pdf.
[77] GAO, Critical Infrastructure Protection: Key Pipeline Security Documents Need to Reflect Current Operating Environment, GAO-19-426, June 2019.
[78] Ibid., pp. 29-30.

Annex in 2020. In addition, according to GAO, TSA plans to publish an update to its Pipeline Security and Incident Recovery Protocol Plan by the end of 2021.[79]

In July 2021, a GAO official testified that TSA had addressed several weaknesses in the management of pipeline security and had fully addressed 12 GAO recommendations identified in the 2018 and 2019 reports. However, according to the testimony, TSA had not fully addressed two cybersecurity-related weaknesses: incomplete information for pipeline risk assessments and aged protocols for responding to pipeline security incidents.[80] With respect to incomplete information, the TSA Administrator subsequently testified that "we oftentimes never have full and complete data, that's very hard to achieve.... [W]e need to move fast ... so we use the best data that we have." However, he agreed with GAO's recommendation and stated that TSA was "working very hard on it."[81]

Issues for Congress

While the federal government has been engaged in various efforts to protect the nation's oil and natural gas pipelines from deliberate cyberattacks since September 11, 2001, questions remain regarding the structure and effectiveness of these efforts. Five specific issues, in particular, have raised concern and may warrant further congressional consideration: (1) TSA's pipeline cybersecurity resources, (2) the nature of federal cybersecurity standards, (3) roles and coordination among federal entities involved in pipeline cybersecurity, (4) uncertainty about cybersecurity threats to the nation's pipeline network, and (5) coordinating a national pipeline strategy.

TSA Pipeline Cybersecurity Staffing Resources

The sufficiency of staff funding and resources to implement the nation's pipeline security program has been a concern of Congress almost since DHS

---

[79] Leslie V. Gordon, June 11, 2021.
[80] Leslie V. Gordon, "Critical Infrastructure Protection: TSA Is Taking Steps to Address Some Pipeline Security Program Weaknesses," written testimony submitted for the Senate Committee on Commerce, Science, and Transportation hearing on "Pipeline Cybersecurity: Protecting Critical Infrastructure," GAO-21-105263, July 27, 2021, pp. 11, 14.
[81] David P. Pekoske, July 27, 2021.

was established. For example, one Senator remarked in 2005 that "aviation security has received 90% of TSA's funds and virtually all of its attention. There is simply not enough being done to address ... pipeline security."[82] At a hearing in April 2010, a Member likewise expressed concern that TSA's pipeline division did not have sufficient staff to carry out a federal pipeline security program on a national scale.[83] According to GAO's 2019 report, TSA itself acknowledged that staffing limitations had prevented the agency from conducting more pipeline security reviews.[84] In February 2019, TSA had five FTE staff in pipeline security, none with "specific cybersecurity expertise," according to the agency.[85]

On June 15, 2021, the TSA Assistant Administrator testified that TSA's pipeline security staffing would increase in FY2021 "to 34 positions working in field operations, headquarters operations, and policy development," although some of these positions had yet to be filled. Of these 34 positions, 6 would be for "specialized cybersecurity personnel," in a new Cybersecurity Operations Support Branch, with another 5 cybersecurity specialists to be hired into the branch in FY2022. TSA's Surface Policy Division also plans to have 9 FTEs in the Cybersecurity Section of its Office of Policy, Plans, and Engagement by the end of FY2021 to "focus on the development of cybersecurity-related policy and guidance for surface transportation security."[86]

The TSA Assistant Administrator also testified that the agency currently has the funding and personnel needed to ensure accountability for pipeline operator cybersecurity.[87] Nonetheless, it is uncertain whether the agency, as currently staffed and structured, could develop and implement new security regulations (if needed), conduct rigorous security plan verification, follow up with effective enforcement, and maintain currency regarding the cybersecurity threat environment.

Developing and implementing more prescriptive cybersecurity regulations could pose a particular challenge to agency resources, depending

---

[82] Sen. Daniel K. Inouye, opening statement before the Senate Committee on Commerce, Science, and Transportation hearing on the President's FY2006 Budget Request for the Transportation Security Administration, February 15, 2005.

[83] Rep. Gus M. Bilirakis, Remarks Before the House Committee on Homeland Security, Subcommittee on Management, Investigations, and Oversight hearing on "Unclogging Pipeline Security: Are the Lines of Responsibility Clear?," Plant City, FL, April 19, 2010.

[84] GAO, December 2018, p. 38.

[85] Sonya T. Proctor, February 26, 2019.

[86] Sonya T. Proctor, June 15, 2021.

[87] Ibid.

upon the process (e.g., directives, rulemaking), nature, and extent of such regulations.

Cybersecurity Standards

There continues to be debate in Congress about the adequacy of a voluntary standards approach to cybersecurity within the pipeline sector (as well as other critical infrastructure sectors). Prior to the May 2021 Colonial Pipeline cyberattack, TSA used a voluntary approach to pipeline security generally, and to cybersecurity specifically, as discussed above. This approach was controversial. For example, as early as 2008, a DOT Inspector General report stated that "TSA's current security guidance is not mandatory and remains unenforceable unless a regulation is issued to require industry compliance."[88] The issue of whether to have voluntary or mandatory standards has arisen often over the last decade. Some stakeholders have advocated for mandatory standards to ensure compliance and others, notably the pipeline industry and TSA, have asserted that the voluntary standards approach has been effective.[89]

TSA has started to move past voluntary compliance. Following the Colonial Pipeline attack, the agency issued its two security directives requiring critical operators to have a cybersecurity coordinator, report incidents, assess cyber vulnerability, and implement prescriptive measures and practices to defend against cyber threats. However, under the TSA's directives, questions may arise about how pipeline operators fulfill their cybersecurity requirements. In particular, there is debate about the relative suitability and efficacy of prescriptive standards versus performance standards in the pipeline sector. Prescriptive standards mandate particular means (e.g., specific types of hardware or software). Performance standards establish goals that entities must achieve (e.g., continuous monitoring) but allow entities to individually decide how to achieve those goals. A voluntary or mandatory standard can be either prescriptive or performance-based.

---

[88] U.S. Dept. of Transportation, Office of Inspector General, May 21, 2008, p. 6. Provisions in the Pipeline Inspection, Protection, Enforcement, and Safety Act of 2006 (P.L. 109-468) required the Inspector General to "address the adequacy of security standards for gas and oil pipelines" (§23(b)(4)).

[89] See, for example, testimony before the Senate Committee on Commerce, Science, and Transportation hearing on "Transportation Security Administration Oversight: Confronting America's Transportation Security Challenges," April 30, 2014.

According to TSA officials, the agency's second directive imposes more prescriptive cybersecurity mitigation requirements on operators. TSA's announcement of the directive stated that it was mandating "urgently needed protections" to "better ensure the pipeline sector takes the steps necessary to safeguard their operations from rising cyber threats."[90] However, some in the pipeline sector have criticized the second directive as overly prescriptive and as having been promulgated under emergency authority without a traditional rulemaking process with more industry input.[91] As TSA evaluates its current security directives for pipelines and considers additional directives or rules, the balance of voluntary vs. mandatory and prescriptive vs. performance standards may continue to be an issue for Congress.

Roles of Federal Entities and Agency Coordination

Some Members of Congress and other stakeholders have questioned whether aspects of the federal program for pipeline security, especially cybersecurity, should be administered by an agency other than TSA. Concerns with TSA have centered on the adequacy of personnel and expertise, industry relationships, and experience with regulatory programs. For example, in 2018, two FERC commissioners asserted that the program should be moved to an agency that "fully comprehends the energy sector and has sufficient resources to address this growing threat." The commissioners specifically proposed DOE as a more "appropriate" place for the program because DOE is the Sector-Specific Agency for energy security and also administers CESER.[92] Other stakeholders have suggested that PHMSA might be a more suitable agency to administer the pipeline security program due to its greater resources, pipeline expertise, long-standing relationships with operators, and existing pipeline safety regulatory program.[93] Still others have expressed support for TSA's continued oversight of pipeline cybersecurity. Among other reasons, they cite the agency's recent expansion of staffing dedicated to pipeline cybersecurity, its collaboration with CISA, and other organizational changes.

---

[90] Department of Homeland Security, July 20, 2021.
[91] Leticia Gonzales, "TSA Adds More Stringent Cybersecurity Requirements for U.S. Natural Gas, Oil Pipelines," Natural Gas Intelligence, July 23, 2021.
[92] Neil Chatterjee and Richard Glick, "Cybersecurity Threats to U.S. Gas Pipelines Call for Stricter Oversight," Axios, June 11, 2018.
[93] See, for example, Blake Sobczak, "Battle Lines Form over Pipeline Cyberthreat," E&E News, July 25, 2019.

Pending legislative proposals pertain to the role of TSA and other federal agencies in pipeline cybersecurity. They seek to recodify TSA's cybersecurity role (e.g., Pipeline Security Act, H.R. 3243) and to require the Secretary of Energy to carry out certain responsibilities for pipeline cybersecurity (e.g., Pipeline and LNG Facility Cybersecurity Preparedness Act, H.R. 3078).

Another bill, the Promoting Interagency Coordination for Review of Natural Gas Pipelines Act (H.R. 1616), would require FERC to consult with TSA in reviewing interstate natural gas pipeline permit applications regarding an applicant's compliance with TSA's pipeline cybersecurity standards and recommendations. Recently enacted measures and actions include passage of the PIPEs Act of 2020 (P.L. 116-260, Division R) reauthorizing PHMSA's pipeline safety program, the FAST Act (P.L. 114-94) authorizing DOE's responsibility for energy delivery cybersecurity, and the 2016 U.S. Coast Guard/NIST partnership on cyber risk management for the transfer of hazardous liquids from marine vessels to onshore pipelines.[94]

During a 2021 budget hearing of the Senate Committee on Energy and Natural Resources with the Secretary of Energy, Senators raised concerns about the multiagency oversight of pipeline cybersecurity.[95] Concerns include the opportunities for gaps and oversight without a single agency in charge. Conversely, other Members have suggested keeping the current multiagency approach since it encourages agencies to focus capabilities on areas where they have the greatest expertise.[96] As Congress further examines federal roles for pipeline cybersecurity, it may evaluate the breadth of agencies' pipeline authorities (e.g., security as a whole, or exclusively cybersecurity), the location in the federal government of cyber-specific capabilities, the capacity of those capabilities, and the mechanisms agencies employ to coordinate capabilities.

---

[94] U.S. Coast Guard, "Maritime Bulk Liquid Transfer Cybersecurity Framework Profile," 2016, at https://www.dco.uscg.mil/Portals/9/CG-FAC/Documents/Maritime_BLT_ CSF.pdf?ver =2017-07-19-070544-223.

[95] U.S. Congress, Senate Committee on Energy and Natural Resources, The President's Budget Request for the Department of Energy for Fiscal Year 2022, 117th Cong., 1st sess., June 15, 2021.

[96] U.S. Congress, House Committee on Homeland Security, Subcommittees on Transportation and Maritime Security, and Cybersecurity, Infrastructure Protection, and Innovation, Cyber Threats in the Pipeline: Lessons from the Federal Response to the Colonial Pipeline Ransomware Attack, 117th Cong., 1st sess., June 15, 2021.

Pipeline Cybersecurity Threat Information

Concerns about the quality and specificity of federal threat information have long been an issue across critical infrastructure sectors.[97] Threat information continues to be a key concern in the case of pipeline cybersecurity.[98] The pipeline industry's cybersecurity assessments rely upon information about cybersecurity threats provided by the federal government and by pipeline operators themselves. The quantity, quality, and timeliness of this threat information are key determinants of which threats pipeline companies protect against, and which security measures are taken. Incomplete or ambiguous threat information—especially from the federal government—may lead to inconsistency in cybersecurity mitigation among pipeline owners, inefficient spending of security resources at facilities, or deployment of security measures against the wrong threat.

Questions for Congress related to pipeline cybersecurity threat information include the following:

- Which agency (or agencies) should be responsible for collecting, analyzing, and/or disseminating threat information?
- Which agency (or agencies) should be responsible for developing mitigating strategies to cybersecurity threats?
- Does the intelligence community need to improve collection about adversary targeting of critical infrastructure?
- How will the government track the disposition of information shared and assess the efficacy of information-sharing programs?
- Is classified information a barrier to information sharing, or is pertinent information able to be disseminated in an unclassified manner?
- Has the cyber risk information-sharing model authorized in the Cybersecurity Act of 2015 (P.L. 114-113, Division N) been successful, or do barriers exist to effective information sharing among sector partners? The model in the act involves sector-wide information sharing through information sharing and analysis organizations.

---

[97] See, for example, Philip Shenon, "Threats and Responses: Domestic Security," New York Times, June 5, 2003, p. A15.

[98] U.S. Congress, House Committee on Homeland Security, *Cyber Threats in the Pipeline: Using Lessons from the Colonial Pipeline Ransomware Attack to Defend Critical Infrastructure*, 117th Cong., 1st sess., June 9, 2021.

Congress examined aspects of these issues during the first session of the 117th Congress. For example, during a hearing of the Senate Committee on Commerce, Science, and Transportation on pipeline cybersecurity, federal officials asserted a need for "trusted and timely" information sharing among both public- and private-sector partners.[99] Also, a hearing by the House Committee on Energy and Commerce highlighted an example of challenges to information sharing: the government may share classified information with a company's executive, but that executive may lack cleared personnel in the company who can then take action on the information because of its classification.[100]

Coordinating a National Pipeline Cybersecurity Strategy

In addition to the specific issues highlighted above, Congress may assess how the various elements of U.S. pipeline cybersecurity and critical infrastructure security will fit together most effectively in the nation's overall strategy to protect critical pipelines. Pipeline security necessarily involves various groups: federal agencies, pipeline associations, large and small pipeline operators, and the broader industrial cybersecurity community. Reviewing how these groups work together to achieve common goals could be an overarching challenge for Congress.

---

[99] U.S. Congress, Senate Committee on Commerce, Science, and Transportation, Pipeline Cybersecurity: Protecting Critical Infrastructure, 117th Cong., 1st sess., July 21, 2021.
[100] U.S. Congress, House Committee on Energy and Commerce, Subcommittee on Energy, FERC Oversight, 117th Cong., 1st sess., July 27, 2021.

Chapter 3

Transportation Cybersecurity: Protecting Planes, Trains, and Pipelines from Cyber Threats*

Committee on Homeland Security

Tuesday, October 26, 2021
U.S. House of Representatives
Subcommittee on Cybersecurity, Infrastructure Protection, and Innovation, and the Subcommittee on Transportation and Maritime Security
Washington, DC.

The subcommittees met, pursuant to notice, at 2:04 p.m., via Webex, Hon. Yvette D. Clarke [Chairwoman of the Subcommittee on Cybersecurity, Infrastructure Protection, and Innovation] presiding.

Present: Representatives Clarke, Watson Coleman, Jackson Lee, Langevin, Titus, Slotkin, Rice, Luria, Torres, Garbarino, Gimenez, Norman, Van Drew, Harshbarger, Miller-Meeks, Clyde, and LaTurner.

Ms. CLARKE. The Committee on Cybersecurity, Infrastructure Protection, and Innovation and the Subcommittee on Transportation and Maritime Security will come to order for today's hearing entitled "Transportation Security: Protecting Planes, Trains, and Pipelines from Cyber Threats."

---

* This is an edited, reformatted and augmented version of Joint Hearing Before the Subcommittee on Cybersecurity, Infrastructure Protection, and Innovation and the Subcommittee on Transportation and Maritime Security of the Committee on Homeland Security, House of Representatives, Publication Serial No. 117–34, dated October 26, 2021.

In: Infrastructure Cybersecurity
Editor: Michael V. Walls
ISBN: 979-8-89113-039-5
© 2023 Nova Science Publishers, Inc.

Without objection, the Chair is authorized to declare the subcommittees in recess at any point.

Let me start by thanking Chairwoman Watson Coleman and Ranking Member Garbarino, Ranking Member Gimenez, and our panel of witnesses for joining us today.

We are here to assess the administration's actions aimed at mitigating the cybersecurity challenges facing the transportation sector. Earlier this year, our subcommittees worked together to evaluate how the Federal Government partners with the private sector to respond to a ransomware attack against Colonial Pipeline which resulted in 5,500 miles of pipeline being shut down.

As panic led to fuel shortages at gas stations along the East Coast and airlines scrambled to find alternative fuel supplies, we learned that, No. 1, attackers infiltrated Colonial Pipeline's business network using a legacy VPN that did not require multifactor authentication; No. 2, the flow of information between Colonial Pipeline, the Cybersecurity and Infrastructure Security Agency, and the Transportation Security Administration was slow, fueled in part by ongoing confusion about which agency was in charge; and, No. 3, despite repeated offers from TSA, Colonial Pipeline had not yet undergone an important security assessment, a validated architecture design review, and did not have a disaster response plan that contemplated a full—the full scope of cyber threats.

Shocked by what we learned during their oversight of Colonial Pipeline and other recent high-profile cyber incidents, Members of Congress have begun to question whether the Federal Government's approach to cybersecurity, which relies primarily on voluntary partnerships, actually works, or whether some security requirements ought to be mandated.

The notion that certain entities should be subject to cybersecurity standard mandates is not new. Almost 10 years ago, President Obama issued Executive Order 13636 on improving critical infrastructure cybersecurity. The Executive Order directed sector risk management agencies to evaluate whether they had sufficient authority to establish cybersecurity requirements for critical infrastructure entities for which a, "cybersecurity incident could reasonably result in catastrophic regional or National effects on a public health or safety, economic security, or National security," and report back to DHS and the White House with what they found.

To the best of my knowledge, no agency suggested they lacked authority to issue such requirements. Nevertheless, for nearly a decade, the Federal Government has continued to pursue security policies that rely primarily on voluntary partnerships with the private sector. That is why the security directives that TSA issued for pipelines and the requirements TSA plans to issue for rail, transit, and aviation deserve such careful attention. They mark a pivotal transition in the Federal Government's approach to cybersecurity. As a representative from Brooklyn, I welcome TSA's renewed interest in improving the cybersecurity posture of the transportation sector. New York City is a transportation hub, home to two major airports, several rail lines, and the largest mass transit system in the Nation. Just 6 months ago, actors reportedly tied to the Chinese Government breached the Metropolitan Transit Authority's network. Fortunately, they did not gain access to operational systems that control rail cars, but I remain concerned about the cybersecurity of mass transit systems generally and MTA's network in particular.

Given the degree to which middle- and low-income people rely on public transportation, a cyberattack affecting mass transit could have a disproportionate impact on these populations. In light of the conversations I have had regarding cybersecurity threats to rail and aviation, I also support TSA's efforts to raise the bar on cybersecurity for these subsectors.

That said, as the Federal approach to securing critical infrastructure evolves, we must get it right. TSA's security directives on pipelines and pending securities directives on trail—excuse me—on transit, rail, and aviation present an opportunity to better understand the administration's security goals, how the security directives align with those goals, and the private sector's ability to effectively implement the directives.

Today, I hope to identify the lessons learned from the roll-out and implementation of the pipeline security directives so we can use them to inform future transportation security directives to ensure that they are buying down risk and yielding the security benefits we expect. More broadly, I hope today's conversation will provide insight into how we can raise the cybersecurity posture across critical infrastructure sectors.

I thank the witnesses for being here today, and I look forward to your testimony.

[The statement of Chairwoman Clarke follows:]

Statement of Chairwoman Yvette D. Clarke

The Subcommittee on Cybersecurity, Infrastructure Protection, and Innovation and the Subcommittee on Transportation and Maritime Security will come to order for today's hearing, titled "Transportation Cybersecurity: Protecting Planes, Trains, and Pipelines from Cyber Threats." Without objection, the Chair is authorized to declare the subcommittees in recess at any point.

Thank you to Chairwoman Watson Coleman, Ranking Member Garbarino, Ranking Member Gimenez, and our panel of witnesses for joining us.

We are here today to assess the administration's actions aimed at mitigating the cybersecurity challenges facing the transportation sector.

Earlier this year, our subcommittees worked together to evaluate how the Federal Government partnered with the private sector to respond to a ransomware attack against Colonial Pipeline, which resulted in 5,500 miles of pipeline being shut down.

As panic led to fuel shortages at gas stations along the East Coast and airlines scrambled to find alternative fuel supplies, we learned that:

- attackers infiltrated Colonial Pipeline's business network using a legacy VPN that did not require multi-factor authentication;
- the flow of information between Colonial Pipeline, the Cybersecurity and Infrastructure Security Agency, and the Transportation Security Administration was slow, fueled in part by on-going confusion about which agency was in charge; and
- despite repeated offers from TSA, Colonial Pipeline had not yet undergone an important security assessment—a Validated Architecture Design Review—and did not have a disaster response plan that contemplated the full scope of cyber threats.

Shocked by what we learned during their oversight of Colonial Pipeline and other recent high-profile cyber incidents, Members of Congress have begun to question whether the Federal Government's approach to cybersecurity—which relies primarily on voluntary partnerships—actually works, or whether some security requirements ought to be mandated.

The notion that certain entities should be subject to cybersecurity standard mandates is not new.

Almost 10 years ago, President Obama issued Executive Order 13636, on Improving Critical Infrastructure Cybersecurity.

The Executive Order directed sector risk management agencies to evaluate whether they had sufficient authority to establish cybersecurity requirements for critical infrastructure entities for which a "cybersecurity incident could reasonably result in catastrophic regional or National effects on public health or safety, economic security, or National security"—and report back to DHS and the White House with what they found.

To the best of my knowledge, no agency suggested they lacked authority to issue such requirements.

Nevertheless, for nearly a decade, the Federal Government has continued to pursue security policies that relied primarily on voluntary partnerships with the private sector.

That's why the security directives that TSA issued for pipelines—and the requirements TSA plans to issue for rail, transit, and aviation—deserve such careful attention. They mark a pivotal transition in the Federal Government's approach to cybersecurity.

As a representative from Brooklyn, I welcome TSA's renewed interest in improving the cybersecurity posture of the transportation sector.

New York City is a transportation hub—home to two major airports, several rail lines, and the largest mass transit system in the country.

Just 6 months ago, hackers reportedly tied to the Chinese government breached Metropolitan Transportation Authority's network.

Fortunately, they did not gain access to operational systems that control rail cars—but I remain concerned about the cybersecurity of mass transit systems, generally, and MTA's network, in particular.

Given the degree to which middle- and low-income people rely on public transportation, a cyberattack affecting mass transit could have a disproportionate impact on these populations.

In light of the conversations I have had regarding cybersecurity threats to rail and aviation, I also support TSA's efforts to raise the bar on cybersecurity for these subsectors.

That said, as the Federal approach to securing critical infrastructure evolves, we must get it right.

TSA's security directives on pipelines—and pending security directives on transit, rail, and aviation—present an opportunity to better understand the administration's security goals, how the security directives align with those goals, and the private sector's ability to effectively implement the directives.

Today, I hope to identify the lessons learned from the rollout and implementation of the pipeline security directives, so we can use them to inform future transportation security directives to ensure that they are buying down risk and yielding the security benefits we expect.

More broadly, I hope today's conversation will provide insight into how we can raise the cybersecurity posture across critical infrastructure sectors.

I thank the witnesses for being here today and I look forward to their testimony.

Ms. CLARKE. The Chair now recognizes the Ranking Member of the Subcommittee on Cybersecurity, Infrastructure Protection, and Innovation, the gentleman from New York, Mr. Garbarino, for an opening statement.

Mr. GARBARINO. Thank you, Chairwoman Clarke and Chairwoman Watson Coleman, for holding this important hearing today. Thank to you my colleague, Ranking Member Gimenez, for his continued leadership on transportation security.

As you know, cybersecurity remains a bipartisan cooperation in Congress. Bringing together these two subcommittees is a continuation of the bipartisan spirit that makes this community function so well. But there remains room for improvement.

This year, the full committee and our Cybersecurity Subcommittee have held several hearings in the aftermath of major cyber incidents to review the state of our Nation's cyber preparedness and assess the overall efficacy of response mechanisms across the Federal Government within various industry sectors. This joint hearing is a great opportunity to continue that work, focusing on the transportation sector which impacts millions of Americans and many of my constituents.

Every day, Americans are already experiencing the impact of a pervasive supply chain crisis. Goods are becoming more expensive and harder to find. Nearly every sector of our economy has been affected by this problem, which is particularly acute in the auto industry. We have already witnessed the impact of a devastating ransomware attack on Colonial Pipeline which led to gas shortages on the East Coast. Imagine a similar attack on a major U.S. port, airline, or major logistics company as the holidays approach. We must ensure that there is a robust partnership between the Department of Homeland Security, particularly the Cybersecurity and Infrastructure Security Agency, the Transportation Security Agency, and the U.S. Coast Guard, and the owners and operators of our transportation systems.

I hope that this hearing reviews the cyber preparedness of our critical transportation systems and how agencies like CISA, TSA, and the Coast Guard can enhance their programs, services, and guidance to best ensure entities can defend and mitigate the threat of cyberattacks.

I am particularly interested in learning more about DHS's use of security directives as a tool for enforcing new security standards. I would like to hear testimony and learn from our witnesses regarding the impact of security directives and how TSA is working with relevant partners to ensure robust industry input because they know their sector best. I would also like to hear from our witnesses on the extent to which industry expertise and feedback is utilized in the creation of these security directives.

Members of this committee, including myself, are actively engaged in crafting mandatory cyber incident reporting legislation to improve CISA's ability into cyber incidents impacting our Nation's critical infrastructure. I thank Chairwoman Clarke for her leadership and partnership on this effort.

I have also been working closely with Ranking Member Katko and Representative Spanberger to introduce bipartisan legislation to authorize the director of CISA to establish a stakeholder-driven transparent process for identifying the owners and operators of our Nation's most critical infrastructure, known as systemically important critical infrastructure.

How can we expect CISA and other sector risk management agencies to prioritize limited services if we don't know what is most critical? It is also incumbent on Congress to ensure such a program includes the appropriate guardrails, guidance, and built-in mechanisms for industry collaboration. Such an important program must be done right. I believe that securing systemically important critical infrastructure strives to these very principles.

I am disappointed that the committee held a mark-up this morning, this legislation was not included, despite months of industry collaboration and attempts to collaborate with the Majority. I hope it comes soon.

I do want to note Representative Langevin's leadership on this important issue and his transparency with the Minority. I look forward to working with him and with you, Chairwoman Clarke, on this legislation to continue the bipartisan nature of our subcommittee.

Last, I will just say that the issue of transportation cybersecurity hits close to home. It was shortly after New York's MTA systems were hacked in April and discovered in June in which Secretary Mayorkas announced intentions to create a new security directive for major rail and aviation entities.

I look forward to learning from our panelists here today about what this committee can do to help TSA, CISA, and the Coast Guard work toward an enhanced public-private partnership with owners and operators of our Nation's transportation system.

Thank you very much, Chairwomen. I yield back.

[The statement of Ranking Member Garbarino follows:]

Statement of Ranking Member Andrew Garbarino

Thank you, Chairwoman Clarke and Chairwoman Watson Coleman for holding this important hearing today. And thank you, Ranking Member Gimenez, for your continued leadership on transportation security.

As you know all, cybersecurity remains an area of bipartisan cooperation in Con gress.

Bringing together these two subcommittees is a continuation of the bipartisan spirit that makes this committee function so well, but there remains room for improvement.

This year, the full committee and our Cybersecurity Subcommittee have held several hearings in the aftermath of major cyber incidents to review the state of our Nation's cyber preparedness and assess the overall efficacy of response mechanisms across the Federal Government and within various industry sectors.

This joint hearing is a great opportunity to continue that work, focusing on the transportation sector, which impacts millions of Americans.

Everyday Americans are already experiencing the impact of a pervasive supply chain crisis. Goods are becoming more expensive and harder to find. Nearly every sector of our economy has been affected by this problem, which is particularly acute in the auto industry.

We have already witnessed the impact of a devastating ransomware attack on Colonial Pipeline, which led to gas shortages on the East Coast. Imagine a similar attack on a major U.S. port, airline, or major logistics company as the holidays approach.

We must ensure there is a robust partnership between the Department of Homeland Security, particularly the Cybersecurity and Infrastructure Security Agency (CISA), the Transportation Security Agency (TSA), and the U.S. Coast Guard and the owners and operators of our transportation systems.

I hope that this hearing reviews the cyber preparedness of our critical transportation systems and how agencies like CISA, TSA, and the Coast Guard can enhance their programs, services, and guidance to best ensure entities can defend and mitigate the threat of cyberattacks.

I am particularly interested in learning more about DHS's use of security directives as a tool for enforcing new security standards.

I would like to hear testimony and learn from our witnesses regarding the impact of security directives, and how TSA is working with relevant partners to ensure robust industry input, because they know their sector best.

I would also like to hear from our witnesses on the extent to which industry expertise and feedback is utilized in the creation of these security directives.

Members of this committee, including myself, are actively engaged in crafting mandatory cyber incident reporting legislation to improve CISA's visibility into cyber incidents impacting our Nation's critical infrastructure. I thank Chairwoman Clarke for her leadership and partnership on this effort.

I've also been working closely with Ranking Member Katko and Rep. Spanberger to introduce bipartisan legislation to authorize the director of CISA to establish a stakeholder-driven, transparent process for identifying the owners and operators of our Nation's most critical infrastructure—known as systemically important critical infrastructure. How can we expect CISA, and other Sector Risk Management Agencies to prioritized limited services if we don't know who is the most critical?

It is also incumbent on Congress to ensure such a program includes the appropriate guard rails, guidance, and built-in mechanisms for industry collaboration, such an important program must be done right. I believe that the Securing Systemically Important Critical Infrastructure Act strives for these very principles. I'm disappointed that the committee held a markup this morning, and this legislation was not included despite months of industry collaboration and attempts to collaborate with the Majority.

I do want to note Rep. Langevin's leadership on this important issue, and his transparency with the Minority. I look forward to working with him, and you Chairwoman Clarke on this legislation, to continue to bipartisan nature of this subcommittee.

Last, I'll just say that the issue of transportation cybersecurity hits close to home. It was shortly after New York's MTA systems were hacked in April, and discovered in June, in which Secretary Mayorkas announced intentions to create a new security directive for major rail and aviation entities.

I look forward to learning from our panelists here today about what his committee can do to help TSA, CISA, and the Coast Guard work toward an enhanced publicprivate partnership with owners and operators of our Nation's transportation system.

Ms. CLARKE. Thank you, Ranking Member Garbarino.

The Chair now recognizes the Chairwoman of the Subcommittee on Transportation and Maritime Security, the gentlelady from New Jersey, Mrs. Bonnie Watson Coleman, for an opening statement.

Mrs. WATSON COLEMAN. Thank you, Chairwoman Clarke. To our Ranking Members Gimenez and Garbarino, thank you for coming together around this very important issue. To our witnesses, thank you for being willing to discuss this critical topic.

I want to be crystal clear. When it comes to transportation cybersecurity, inaction is not an option. When gas stops flowing due to a cyberattack, it doesn't just impact the pipeline owner; it means Americans struggle to fill up their tanks. If hackers succeed in bringing down a plane or derailing a train, it is not an airline or railroad that would pay the steepest price. Indeed, the real cost would be borne by the passengers injured or even killed.

Simply put, when you own critical infrastructure, people's lives and livelihoods depend on your cybersecurity. Yet despite the stakes, most transportation operators currently have no obligation to meet even baseline cybersecurity standards.

The status quo is dangerous. We are all familiar with the attack on Colonial Pipeline, but just this year, hackers have also targeted New York's MTA, as stated, the Massachusetts ferry system, the Port of Houston, one of the largest repositories of airline passenger records, a leading pipeline maintenance company, and global freight railroads. The list goes on.

Unquestionably, our Nation's transportation systems are facing a crisis. Fortunately, TSA has begun the process of requiring critical operators to take basic cybersecurity precautions. The recent cybersecurity directors for pipelines and Secretary Mayorkas' announcement of forthcoming requirements for rail, transit, and aviation are justified, necessary, and an important first step. But more action is even needed.

For instance, TSA must ensure all transportation moves are covered. Particularly as vehicles become increasingly connected and autonomous, the cybersecurity of motor carriers and busses cannot be forgotten. Meanwhile, the Coast Guard needs to hold ferries, ports, and other maritime systems to similar standards.

There is also the question of implementation and enforcement. If an operator proposes an alternative procedure that maintains robust cybersecurity, TSA needs to provide timely, substantive feedback.

By the same token, if operators fail to comply, leaving our Nation's critical infrastructure vulnerable to attack, TSA must have the resources to enforce the rules. Ultimately, TSA should pursue traditional notice-and-comment regulations so that stakeholders can offer meaningful input.

But these conversations around implementation shouldn't distract from the fundamental fact: There is no substitute for mandatory transportation cybersecurity requirements like those that are announced by TSA and Secretary Mayorkas.

While many operators employ best practices, invest in cybersecurity talent, and coordinate with Government voluntarily, some cut corners and put us all at risk. Without requirements, there is nothing to compel those companies to improve. That is a prospect we cannot take lightly, because in the 21st Century, physical security and cybersecurity are two sides of the same coin.

Historically, to hijack a plane, you had to clear TSA's checkpoint and then breach the cockpit. Today, it may be possible to hijack a plane by hacking it. The same is true for railroads, subways, and other modes. Cameras and guards are no match for a hacker seeking to control or derail a train.

This isn't science fiction. This is the future, and cybersecurity requirements for all modes are the way to prepare for it, as well as tackle today's immediate threats, such as ransomware and state-sponsored data theft. A recent study found that only 60 percent of transit agencies have a cybersecurity preparedness program in place. The surge in cyberattacks against railroads, airlines, airports, and maritime assets suggest an equally grim picture in these modes.

This is our moment to ensure that every transportation operator in America prepares themselves for 21st Century threats. We can't wait until a hacked plane falls from the sky or a breached railroad gridlocks our Nation's supply chain to take action. I look forward to hearing from our panel today about what can be done to shore up the cyber defenses of our transportation system.

Again, I thank the witnesses for joining us. Madam Chairwoman, I yield back.

[The statement of Chairwoman Watson Coleman follows:]

Statement of Chairwoman Bonnie Watson Coleman

Thank you, Chairwoman Clarke, and thank you to our witnesses for joining us today to discuss this critical topic.

I want to be crystal clear: When it comes to transportation cybersecurity, inaction isn't an option.

When gas stops flowing due to a cyberattack, it doesn't just impact the pipeline's owner. It means Americans struggle to fill up their tanks.

If hackers succeed in bringing down a plane or derailing a train, it's not an airline or railroad that would pay the steepest price. The real cost would be borne by the passengers injured or killed.

Simply put, when you own critical infrastructure, people's lives and livelihoods depend on your cybersecurity. Yet despite the stakes, most transportation operators currently have no obligation to meet even baseline cybersecurity standards.

The status quo is dangerous. We're all familiar with the attack on Colonial Pipeline, but just this year, hackers have also targeted New York's MTA, the Massachusetts ferry system, the Port of Houston, one of the largest depositories of airline passenger records, a leading pipeline maintenance company, and global freight railroads. The list goes on.

Unquestionably, our Nation's transportation systems are facing a crisis. Fortunately, TSA has begun the process of requiring critical operators to take basic cybersecurity precautions.

The recent cybersecurity directives for pipelines—and Secretary Mayorkas' announcement of forthcoming requirements for rail, transit, and aviation—are justified, necessary, and an important first step. But more action is needed.

For instance, TSA must ensure all transportation modes are covered. Particularly as vehicles become increasingly connected and autonomous, the cybersecurity of motor-carriers and buses cannot be forgotten. Meanwhile, the Coast Guard needs to hold ferries, ports, and other maritime systems to similar standards.

There's also the question of implementation and enforcement. If an operator proposes an alternative procedure that maintains robust cybersecurity, TSA needs to provide timely, substantive feedback.

By the same token, if operators fail to comply—leaving our Nation's critical infrastructure vulnerable to attack—TSA must have the resources to enforce the rules.

And ultimately, TSA should pursue traditional notice-and-comment regulations so stakeholders can offer meaningful input.

But these conversations around implementation shouldn't distract from a fundamental fact: There's no substitute for mandatory transportation cybersecurity requirements, like those announced by TSA and Secretary Mayorkas.

While many operators employ best practices, invest in cybersecurity talent, and coordinate with Government voluntarily, some cut corners and put us all at risk. Without requirements, there is nothing to compel those companies to improve.

That's a prospect we cannot take lightly, because in the 21st Century, physical security and cybersecurity are two sides of the same coin.

Historically, to hijack a plane, you had to clear TSA's checkpoint and then breach the cockpit. Today, it may be possible to hijack a plane by hacking it.

The same is true for railroads, subways, and other modes. Cameras and guards are no match for a hacker seeking to control or derail a train.

This isn't science fiction. This is the future, and cybersecurity requirements for all modes are the way to prepare for it, as well as tackle today's immediate threats—such as ransomware and state-sponsored data theft.

A recent study found that only 60 percent of transit agencies have a cybersecurity preparedness program in place, and the surge in cyberattacks against railroads, airlines, airports, and maritime assets suggests an equally grim picture in those modes.

This is our moment to ensure that every transportation operator in America prepares themselves for 21st Century threats. We can't wait until a hacked plane falls from the sky or a breached railroad gridlocks our Nation's supply chain to take action.

I look forward to hearing from our panel today about what can be done to shore up the cyber defenses of our transportation systems.

Again, I thank the witnesses for joining us, and I yield back.

Ms. CLARKE. I thank the gentlelady from New Jersey.

The Chair now recognizes the Ranking Member of the Subcommittee on Transportation and Maritime Security, the gentleman from Florida, Mr. Gimenez, for an opening statement.

Mr. GIMENEZ. Thank you, Chairwoman Clarke and Watson Coleman, for holding this important hearing today, and to Ranking Member Garbarino as well. I am glad that we can bring these two subcommittees together to discuss how to protect our vital aviation service, transportation, and maritime systems from cyber threats. I know first-hand from my time as mayor of Miami-Dade County how important these systems are to the flow of people and goods and the overall health of our economy. As we are seeing right now with supply chain challenges and the increasing prices in everyday goods, keeping our transportation system operating at a high level is imperative.

The recent ransomware attack on Colonial Pipeline only served to highlight what owners and operators of these critical infrastructure systems already knew: A significant cyber incident has enormous ramifications to their systems and can cripple the goods and services that our Nation needs.

Transportation system owners and operators have enhanced their cybersecurity practices and real-time information sharing over the years, but there is always more that can be done to strengthen our defenses and it is imperative that we do so. As TSA moves forward with new cybersecurity directives for aviation, rail, and mass transit in the next few weeks, it is important that industry is fully consulted as these requirements are drafted and implemented.

The owners and operators know their systems the best and what is workable. Having a strong public-private partnership as new cyber requirements are imposed in the transportation sector is key. I look forward to hearing from the witnesses today on their perspectives on how to strengthen cybersecurity throughout our transportation system.

Madam Chairwoman, I yield back.

[The statement of Ranking Member Gimenez follows:]

Statement of Ranking Member Carlos Gimenez

Thank you, Chairwomen Clarke and Watson Coleman, for holding this important hearing today. And to Ranking Member Garbarino as well. I'm glad that we can bring these two subcommittees together to discuss how to protect our vital aviation, surface transportation, and maritime systems from cyber threats.

I know first-hand from my time as Mayor of Miami-Dade County how important these systems are to the flow of people and goods and the overall health of our economy. As we're seeing right now with supply chain challenges and the increasing prices in everyday goods, keeping our transportation systems operating at a high level is imperative.

The recent ransomware attack on Colonial Pipeline only served to highlight what owners and operators of these critical infrastructure systems already knew—a significant cyber incident has enormous ramifications to their systems and can cripple the goods and services that our Nation relies on.

Transportation system owners and operators have enhanced their cybersecurity practices and real-time information sharing over the years, but there is always more that can be done to strengthen our defenses.

As TSA moves forward with new cybersecurity directives for aviation, rail, and mass transit in the next few weeks, it's important that industry is fully consulted as these requirements are drafted and implemented. The owners and operators know their systems the best and what is workable. Having a strong public-private partnership as new cyber requirements are imposed in the transportation sector is key.

I look forward to hearing from the witnesses today on their perspectives of how to strengthen cybersecurity throughout our transportation systems.

Madam Chairwoman, I yield back.

Ms. CLARKE. I thank the Ranking Member from Florida, the gentleman, Mr. Gimenez, for his statement.

Members are also reminded that the committee will operate according to the guidelines laid out by the Chairman and Ranking Member in their February 3 colloquy regarding remote procedures.

Member statements may also be included for the record.

[The statements of Chairman Thompson and Honorable Jackson Lee follow:]

Statement of Chairman Bennie G. Thompson

Thank you, Chairwomen Clarke and Watson Coleman, for holding today's hearing, and thank you to our panelists for being here with us.

Today's hearing occurs amid a shifting conversation on how to secure our Nation's transportation systems from cyberattacks.

The Transportation Security Administration has long relied on voluntary collaboration with industry partners to develop and implement cybersecurity measures.

The ransomware attack on Colonial Pipeline and the ensuing gas shortage earlier this year tested the effectiveness of this approach and highlighted the devastating potential effects of a successful cyberattack on transportation systems.

In the aftermath of the attack, the Biden administration moved swiftly to mandate cybersecurity requirements for owners and operators of critical pipelines through two security directives issued by the TSA, with support from CISA.

Over time, TSA will replace these security directives with full notice-and-comment regulations, marking the start of a new regulatory scheme for securing the transportation sector from cyberattacks.

Earlier this month, Secretary Mayorkas announced that TSA will also expand this mandatory approach to other modes of transportation by issuing new cybersecurity requirements for rail, transit, and aviation.

Indeed, while the attack on Colonial Pipeline dominated the headlines, it is far from the only recent cyberattack we have seen targeting transportation systems.

From the subway system in New York City to the Port of Houston, we have seen cyberattacks attempted across all modes of transportation.

I commend the Biden administration for taking the bold steps needed to address these emerging threats.

As DHS embarks upon this new approach, it must act deliberately to ensure its mandates deliver the intended security results.

First, TSA must work in close collaboration with CISA and industry experts to develop requirements that are intelligence-based, actionable, and crafted to achieve the greatest security benefit.

TSA must focus its enforcement efforts on desired outcomes and work with stakeholders to provide flexibility in how regulated parties achieve those outcomes.

Second, DHS must develop a plan for developing the cybersecurity expertise and resources it will need at TSA and CISA to carry out robust outreach and enforcement efforts—not just for the immediate implementation of new requirements, but as a regular way of doing business going forward.

Congress will need to fully fund these efforts, and I look forward to working with my colleagues to deliver the necessary resources.

Finally, as DHS considers plans for securing other critical infrastructure sectors from cyberattacks, the transportation sector may serve as a model for the prospect of mandating cybersecurity measures.

DHS must be transparent with Congress, stakeholders, and the public about its successes and failures.

Consistently evaluating the effectiveness of security efforts will be key to fixing what may not be working well and to considering whether to apply what does work well more broadly across critical infrastructure sectors.

I look forward to discussing these topics with our witnesses today, and I yield back.

Statement of Honorable Sheila Jackson Lee

I want to thank Congresswoman Yvette Clarke, Chair of the Cybersecurity, Infrastructure Protection and Innovation Subcommittee; and Congresswoman Bonnie Watson Coleman, Chair of the Transportation and Maritime Security Subcommittee and the respective Ranking Members of these committees Congressman Andrew Garbarino and Congressman Carlos A. Gimenez for holding today's hearing on "Transportation Cybersecurity: Protecting Planes, Trains, and Pipelines from Cyber Threats."

I thank today's witnesses for their service to their Nation; and I look forward to their testimony:

- Suzanne Spaulding, senior adviser, Center for Strategic and International Studies and former under secretary, National Protection and Programs Directorate;
- Patty Cogswell, strategic advisor, Guidehouse, and former deputy administrator, Transportation Security Administration;
- Jeffrey Troy, president & chief executive officer, Aviation Information Sharing and Analysis Center and former deputy assistant director, Cyber Division, Federal Bureau of Investigation; and
- Scott Dickerson, executive director, Maritime Transportation System Information Sharing and Analysis Center (MTS–ISAC) (Minority witness).

Today's hearing affords Members an opportunity to engage with former Federal cybersecurity and transportation security officials about the current state of cybersecurity across all modes of transportation, as well as recent and forthcoming regulatory actions to enhance transportation cybersecurity.

I look forward to learning more about how the Transportation Security Administration (TSA), Cybersecurity and Infrastructure Security Agency (CISA), the broader law enforcement, and intelligence communities, and transportation owners and operators can address the need for increased cybersecurity preparedness across the transportation sector.

Today's hearing is an important opportunity to view the cyber threat from a realworld perspective.

The threat is not limited to telecommunications, banking, transportation, health care, or critical infrastructure because of omnipresent and ubiquitous nature of attacks.

The Solar Wind attack was an equal opportunity abuser to any network that it invaded.

Colonial Pipeline was just one victim in a long line of victims, which ended with the consumer who curtailed travel plans due the impact on gasoline availability due to the attack.

Any networked device can be a vector for an attack, no matter how small.

The age of hyper-connectivity is upon us and we are not prepared to protect devices that are by design linked to share data traffic. Cybersecurity is not something you can see or actively prove—it is established by each moment of each day that a network or computing device remains free of breaches by adversaries.

For too long the policy of local and Federal law enforcement was that some cyber crimes were too insignificant to waste limited resources on to investigate, conduct arrests, or prosecute—this must change.

We know from our work on this committee that determined adversaries will spare little to succeed in breaching U.S. networks even small efforts provide valuable insights that are applied to increase the likelihood of success for much more damaging attacks.

The goal of cybersecurity throughout the Federal Government must be to block adversaries when it is possible, detect and eradicate them quickly when it is not, and impose consequences to raise the costs and deter malicious behavior in cyber space.

For 4 years, Federal efforts to raise the National cybersecurity posture— across Federal networks, State and local governments, and the private sector— were stunted by a lack of steady, consistent leadership from the White House, leaving agencies to pursue piecemeal approaches to cybersecurity.

Congressional efforts to address the weaknesses in Federal cybersecurity include several Jackson Lee bills that comprise the following measures introduced in the 117th Congress:

- H.R. 119—Cyber Defense National Guard Act, which requires the Office of the Director of National Intelligence to report to Congress regarding the feasibility of establishing a Cyber Defense National Guard that may be activated during emergencies that affect the cybersecurity of the Nation or critical infrastructure.
- H.R. 118—Cyber Vulnerability Disclosure Reporting Act, requires the Department of Homeland Security to submit a report describing the policies and procedures developed to coordinate the disclosure of cyber vulnerabilities. The report shall describe instances when these policies and procedures were used to disclose cyber vulnerabilities in the previous year. Further, the report shall mention the degree to which the disclosed information was acted upon by stakeholders.
- H.R. 57, the DHS Cybersecurity Asset Protection of Infrastructure under "Terrorist Attack Logistical Structure Act" or the CAPITALS Act, which requires the Department of Homeland Security (DHS) to report to Congress on the feasibility of establishing a DHS Civilian Cyber Defense National Resource.

The goals of the Jackson Lee legislative efforts during the 116th Congress were to raise the baseline cybersecurity posture across the Federal and work with the private sector to reduce avoidable, opportunistic attacks and to refocus talent, time, and resources on preventing, detecting, and eliminating more sophisticated attacks. Raising the Nation's baseline cybersecurity posture will require a systemic, whole-of-Government approach to cybersecurity.

The private sector has 85 percent of the Nation's critical infrastructure and much of it has some connectivity to the internet, which means they cannot adequately protect these National assets.

The vulnerabilities in computing technology from the most complex systems to the smallest devices are often found in its software.

This was true in the early 1990's when the first desktop computing technology was produced.

Desktop computing devices were quickly adopted for business and Government use.

The market and regulatory forces that should have forced security and safety improvements on computing technology never developed due to interference from Congress and the courts that excused or deflected culpability for known computing technology errors or omissions in product development or manufacturing that left systems open to attack.

The last defense for computing technology and systems are the concrete steps that organization, companies, and agencies can take to secure their computing assets; and business continuity measures that can be in place to allow meaningful recovery of operations should a successful cyberattack occur.

Business continuity refers to the capability of an organization to continue the delivery of products or services at acceptable levels following a disruptive incident, and business continuity planning or business continuity and resiliency planning is the process of creating systems of prevention and recovery to deal with potential threats to operations.

To survive in the current high-risk computing landscape both Government and private-sector entities must engage in risk mitigation strategies that assess operations from top to bottom to identify potential cyber threats and risk vectors.

This assessment should include both internal and external threats that could compromise business continuity.

Some risks are firmly within an organization's ability to control, such as the controls they implement to secure data and systems.

Continuity planning is also firmly under the control of organizations, and to not invest in proven strategies to survive a cyberattack, is not only irresponsible on the part of owners—but it creates unacceptable risks for their employees, customers, and investors.

I introduced the Cybersecurity Vulnerability Remediation Act was introduced and passed the House during the 115th and 116th Congresses and has been updated again in the 117th Congress to meet the ever-evolving nature of cyber threats faced by Federal and private-sector information systems and our Nation's critical infrastructure.

This bill goes significantly further than the first Cybersecurity Vulnerability bill that I introduced in the 115th Congress, to address the instance of Zero Day Events that can lead to catastrophic cybersecurity failures of information and computing systems.

The ANS to H.R. 2980 responds to the recent cyberattacks on America's private sector and establishes the Federal Government as having a major role in fighting cyberattacks that target Government agencies and the private-sector critical infrastructure.

H.R. 2980, the Cybersecurity Vulnerability Remediation Act:

- Changes the Department of Homeland Security (DHS) definition of security vulnerability to include cybersecurity vulnerability,
- Provides the plan to fix known cybersecurity vulnerabilities,
- Gives the Department of Homeland Security the tools to know more about ransomware attacks and ransom payments, and
- Creates greater transparency on how DHS will defend against and mitigate cybersecurity vulnerabilities and lays the road map for preparing the private sector to better prepare for and mitigate cyberattacks.

The bill requires a report that can include a Classified annex, which I strongly recommend to the Secretary of DHS so that it can be available should the agency elect to engage private-sector entities in a discussion on cyberattacks and breaches targeting critical infrastructure.

This bill is needed because the Nation's dependence on networked computing makes us vulnerable to cyber threats.

In 30 years, the world has gone from one divided by oceans to one that is interconnected through the internet.

An interconnected world has brought us closer together, created new opportunities for business, and citizen engagement, while at the same time given new tools to those who may wish to cause harm using cyberattacks.

In cyber space an attack against one entity or device can devolve into an attack against many.

The work that must be done to secure critical infrastructure from cybersecurity vulnerabilities that include oil and gas pipelines; the electric grid, water treatment facilities, and other privately-held infrastructure must occur with much more order and purposefulness.

The consolidation of cybersecurity for both the .gov domain and for the private sector is now under the jurisdiction of the Committee on Homeland Security was is an important step to better coordinating domestic cybersecurity.

The Need to Take Action

Ransomware is a form of cyber crime where criminal actors compromise a victim's computer systems, preventing access or threatening to release sensitive information if the victim does not provide a ransom payment.

In recent years, the number of ransomware attacks has increased significantly, affecting school districts, police departments, hospitals, and numerous businesses, among others.

In 2020, an estimated 2,400 governments, hospitals, and school districts were victims of ransomware attacks in the United States.

Victims made an estimated $350 million in ransomware payments in 2020, with an average payment of $312,493.

In the first quarter of 2021, the average monetary demand associated with a ransomware attack increased to $220,298, up 43 percent from the previous quarter. While many businesses suffer significant losses due to disruptions from ransomware and the cost of remediation or making ransom payments, when criminals groups target Government entities or other critical infrastructure, the effects can pose significant risks to public safety.

For example, there were 560 ransomware attacks on U.S. health care facilities in 2020, in some cases causing delays in treatment for serious illnesses.

In a growing number of ransomware attacks, the perpetrators engage in "double extortion" where they threaten to release sensitive data publicly if a ransom payment is not made.

Last week, the Washington, DC police department was hit by a ransomware attack that included the release of detailed background reports on 5 current or former police officers and the threat to release files publicly.

Ransomware can be delivered in various ways, the majority of which utilize email. Ransomware is real, but computers aren't infected just by opening emails anymore.

Just opening an email to view it is safe now—although attachments & links in the email can still be dangerous to open.

While it is not always possible to prevent a successful attack, engaging in general security best practices and implementing effective email protection can drastically reduce your risk.

The SolarWinds attack was a wake-up call on any notion that some companies are more trustworthy than others because a trusted software source was the cause of the company's 18,000 customers downloading a compromised version of Orion.

Nearly 40 Federal agencies downloaded the compromised SolarWinds Orion update, but evidence of further compromise has only been detected at 9 Federal agencies to date. Agencies that downloaded the compromised Orion update continue to hunt for indicators of compromise.

It is important to note that about 30 percent of both Government and non-Government victims of the Russian cyber campaign had no direct connection with SolarWinds.

According to news reports, hackers also breached networks by "exploiting known bugs in software products, by guessing on-line passwords and by capitalizing on a variety of issues in the way Microsoft Corp.'s cloud-based software is configured." Bugs can also be called Zero Day Events that if exploited could cost significant disruption in the function of application or services that rely in computers or remote computing services.

The committee recently took action to address the lack of Federal law requiring private entities to report cybersecurity incidents, there is little public information on the number of victims that installed the infected versions of SolarWinds Orion or experienced second-stage intrusions.

The Cybersecurity and Infrastructure Security Agency should be empowered to more effectively coordinate and lead interagency cybersecurity and risk management activities that coordinate functions among critical infrastructure stakeholders.

Congress should provide CISA the authorities and budget that match its mission. Over the past decade, the private sector has raised fair concerns about the value of many Federal cybersecurity programs and has used its concerns as an excuse for not fully participating, to the detriment of National cybersecurity efforts.

That must stop. The private sector has an important role to play to improve the Nation's cybersecurity posture and must step up.

Solving this cybersecurity challenge will require creativity from policy makers as we seek out new strategies to bolster security efforts for Federal and private-sector networks.

I look forward the asking questions of today's witnesses.

Ms. CLARKE. I now welcome our panel of witnesses. Ms. Suzanne Spaulding is a senior advisor to the Center for Strategic and International Studies. Before that, Ms. Spaulding served as the under secretary for the Department of Homeland Security's National Protection and Programs Directorate, which Congress redesignated as CISA in 2018.

Next we have Ms. Patricia Cogswell, a senior strategic advisor for the National Security at Guidehouse, who served as the deputy administrator for the Transportation Security Administration from 2018 through 2020.

I would also like to welcome Mr. Jeffrey Troy, the president and CEO of the Aviation Information Sharing and Analysis Center, or the Aviation ISAC. Prior to the Aviation ISAC, Mr. Troy served as a deputy assistant director of the FBI's Cyber Division.

Finally, we will hear from Mr. Scott Dickerson, the executive director of the Maritime Transportation System Information Sharing and Analysis Center, or the MTS–ISAC.

Without objection, the witnesses' full statements will be inserted in the record.

I now ask each witness to summarize her or his statement for 5 minutes, beginning with Ms. Spaulding.

Ms. Spaulding, I think you have to unmute.

Statement of Suzanne Spaulding, Senior Adviser, Homeland Security, International Security Program, Center for Strategic & International Studies; Former Under Secretary, National Protection and Programs Directorate

Ms. SPAULDING. Madam Chairwoman, can you hear me at this point?
Ms. CLARKE. Yes, I can.
Ms. SPAULDING. Excellent. All right. Thank you.

Chairwomen, Ranking Members, and Members of the committee, thank you for this opportunity to testify today in this joint hearing on TSA directives aimed at ensuring the security and resilience of the aviation, rail, and pipeline sectors against significant cyber incidents.

As the former under secretary at the Department of Homeland Security, where I led what is now called the Cybersecurity and Infrastructure Security Agency, and as a member of the Congressionally-created Cyberspace Solarium Commission, and even going back to my involvement with the Commission on Cybersecurity for the 44th President, which was run out of my current organization, CSIS, I have always favored voluntary market-based solutions to cybersecurity, as they are generally more efficient and flexible. However, I have reluctantly had to conclude that we cannot rely upon markets alone to ensure the continuity of Nationally-critical functions upon which the American public relies.

First, the purely voluntary approach simply has not gotten us to where we need to be, despite decades of effort. The threat is evolving much more quickly than our defense. Even in these key sectors where there has been significant progress on cyber, there is still a need to ensure continued investment across all vital assets. Even in a perfect market, there are external impacts on society and the Nation from inadequate cybersecurity that will simply not be captured in a business' bottom line or their calculation of return on investment.

Externalities have long justified regulation and mandates such as with pollution and highway safety. This is the thinking behind a number of recommendations from the Cyberspace Solarium Commission.

First, we looked at ways to improve the performance of relevant markets, including by providing better market incentives, greater transparency, more information, to improve the cybersecurity behavior of firms. But the Solarium Commission too ultimately concluded that the market alone was not going to be sufficient to provide the level of security and resilience that is urgently needed for the most important elements of our infrastructure, particularly with what the Solarium calls systemically important critical infrastructure.

We recommended creating a transparent methodology for identifying these most critical systems and assets and then building a closer relationship between the Federal Government and the firms that own and operate these systems. The Government should offer a suite of benefits, like improved intelligence sharing and operational support, but industries should also accept burdens, like requirements for security behavior and enhanced incident reporting. Consistent with this thinking, I believe it is appropriate for TSA to use its existing authority to put basic requirements in place for the most critical assets in these three sectors. The details will be important. But as described, these directives seem like a step in the right direction. Collaboration with industry will continue to be an imperative as TSA further develops these directives and perhaps follow-on regulations.

Industry has a level of expertise that will be essential in understanding what needs to be done. It must be at the table to help craft directives that are ambitious but achievable, and Government must invite them early enough in the process to allow them to make a meaningful contribution. In addition, those who depend upon these critical sectors should also make their voices heard in this process.

Moreover, requirements should be informed by an awareness of the tools and technologies that are available to help these asset owners and operators gain visibility into their information technology and operational technology systems, detect malicious activity, and respond quickly and effectively.

To encourage continued innovation in this area, Government should lean toward open, performance-based standards that are technology-neutral and vendor-agnostic. Any new regulations should draw on existing guidelines, standards, and best practices. They should be harmonized with requirements in other sectors, particularly as between pipeline and electric sectors for which there is often significant overlap.

Finally, Congress needs to ensure that DHS has provided the resources necessary to effectively implement and monitor these mandates and continue its equally important voluntary work.

Time is not on our side. The threat environment grows more dangerous with each passing day. We should not wait for a tragedy caused by malicious cyber activity in one of these vital sectors before we take necessary action. The proposed TSA directives reflect a growing body of evidence that the risk of serious disruptions to critical infrastructure is not potential or in the future. It is here now, and it requires an urgent response.

Thank you, and I look forward to your questions. [The prepared statement of Ms. Spaulding follows:]

Prepared Statement of Suzanne Spaulding

Chairwoman Clarke, Chairwoman Watson Coleman, Ranking Member Garbarino, Ranking Member Gimenez, and distinguished Members of the subcommittees, thank you for this opportunity to testify today in this joint hearing on the important issue of ensuring the security and resilience of the aviation, rail, and pipeline sectors against significant disruption from malicious cyber activity.

The safety and security of these 3 sectors falls under the Transportation Security Administration (TSA) at the Department of Homeland Security (DHS). This Spring, following a ransomware incident at Colonial Pipeline that disrupted fuel deliveries along the East Coast and led to panic buying, long lines, and higher prices at gas stations, TSA issued a security directive mandating that certain pipeline owner/operators—those deemed by TSA to be most critical—assess whether their current operations are consistent with TSA's Guidelines on cybersecurity, identify any gaps and remediation measures, and report the results to TSA and others. This was followed in July 2021 with an additional cybersecurity directive mandating implementation of cybersecurity mitigation measures; development of Cybersecurity Contingency Response Plans in the event of an incident; and an annual cybersecurity architecture design review, among other things.

Recently, the Secretary of Homeland Security announced that DHS would be coming out with similar mandates covering critical U.S. airport operators, passenger aircraft operators, and all cargo aircraft operators, as well as "higher-risk" railroad and rail transit assets.[1]

The pipeline directives have not been publicly released and the aviation and rail directives are still under development. However, they have generally been described as prescribing a relatively basic level of cybersecurity measures and plans for incident response. The latter, planning and exercising incident response to reduce the impact of a successful hack is one of the most important, and often underappreciated, elements of managing cyber risk.

The details will be important but, as described, these directives seem like a step in the right direction. Moving forward, TSA will need to operate collaboratively with these sectors to ensure that the requirements and time lines drive toward actual improvements in security and resilience. No directives or regulations will achieve perfect security. This is an exercise in risk management, not risk elimination, which is why planning for incident response is so crucial. The objective should be to ensure that the relevant industries are putting in place a common baseline of measures to strengthen the security and resilience of the highest-risk assets.

As the former Under Secretary at the Department of Homeland Security leading what is now called the Cybersecurity and Infrastructure Security

---

[1] https://thehill.com/policy/cybersecurity/575580-tsa-to-issue-regulations-to-secure-rail-aviation-groups-against-cyber?rl=1.

Agency (CISA), as a member of the Congressionally-created Cyberspace Solarium Commission (CSC), and going back to my involvement with the Commission on Cybersecurity for the 44th President, which was run out of my current organization, the Center for Strategic and International Studies (CSIS), I have always favored voluntary, market-based solutions to cybersecurity. Markets are generally more efficient and, important for such a dynamic area as cyber, nimbler. However, over the last couple of years, I have reluctantly had to conclude that we cannot rely upon markets alone to ensure the continuity of Nationally-critical functions upon which the American public relies. I think there are several reasons for this.

The first is that the purely voluntary approach has not gotten us where we need to be, despite decades of effort. There has been significant progress and a growing level of maturity in industry and in Government on cyber, including in the sectors under discussion today. All three, aviation, rail, and pipelines, have worked collaboratively with DHS over the years to improve their physical and cybersecurity. But the threat is evolving much more quickly than our defense. There is an urgency to addressing this risk to the American public that the market simply cannot address fast enough.

One reason the market has not fully addressed this challenge is the paucity of information. Markets need information to function effectively. For example, information about the scale, scope, and cost of inadequate cybersecurity is needed to drive a demand signal that would prompt appropriate levels of investment and balance the "first-to-market" imperative. Yet, since most cyber incidents are not reported, and those that are do not provide details on costs, this information is lacking. Furthermore, such information is needed to calculate the return on investment (ROI) for security measures. Without it, security professionals often have a hard time convincing management to make needed investments.

Even in a perfect market, there are external impacts on society and the Nation from inadequate cybersecurity, particularly in assets that control essential functions, that will not be captured in a businesses' bottom line or ROI. Externalities have long justified regulation and mandates, such as with pollution and highway safety. In the case of pipelines, rail, and aviation, the potential risks to public health and safety, as well as the potential for cascading economic consequences, calls for a Government role.

This is the thinking behind a number of the recommendations from the Cyberspace Solarium Commission. First, we looked at ways to improve the performance of relevant markets, including by providing better market incentives to improve the cybersecurity behavior of firms. Mandatory reporting of relevant cyber incidents can fill critical information gaps, particularly if paired with the establishment of a Bureau of Cyber Statistics. Bolstering the capabilities of cyber insurance underwriters can help that industry play the role it does in other risk categories to encourage appropriate investments in security and safety.

In addition to nudging firms in the sector toward better cybersecurity behavior, the Federal Government can do more to help these firms make better purchasing decisions regarding the security of the products and services they deploy as part of their business. More Government-sponsored security testing of critical technologies and applications—like industrial control systems—can help firms understand the security characteristics of the devices they deploy. The CSC recommended the creation of Government-sponsored critical technology security centers at places like Federally-funded research and development centers or National labs to fill this gap. Similarly, a clearer ecosystem of cybersecurity product certifications would allow procurement specialists at critical firms in the sector to more easily price security into their purchasing decisions and manage their supply chain risk.

But the CSC, too, ultimately concluded that the market was not going to be sufficient to provide the level of security and resilience that is urgently needed for the most important elements of our infrastructure, particularly what CSC calls Systemically Important Critical Infrastructure. The Solarium recommended creating a robust and transparent methodology for identifying these most critical systems and assets and then building a closer relationship between SICI firms and the Federal Government through a suite of benefits—like improved intelligence sharing and operational support—but also burdens—like requirements for security behavior and enhanced incident reporting.

Consistent with this thinking, I believe it is appropriate for TSA to use its existing authority to put basic requirements in place for the most critical assets in these three sectors. That said, the process is important. According to testimony from Kimberly Denbow Managing Director, Security & Operations American Gas Association, in front of this committee in September in support of the legislation to mandate cyber incident reporting across critical infrastructure, "The TSA Pipeline Group has been the epitome of innovation—leveraging the infrastructure subject matter expertise of pipeline operators, partnering with CISA and Idaho National Labs for inhouse industrial control system cybersecurity knowledge, and collaborating with the Department of Transportation's Pipeline and Hazardous Materials Safety Administration (PHMSA) on cybersecurity reviews of control centers. AGA helped champion the CISA/TSA Pipeline Cybersecurity Initiative and promoted effortlessly the Pipeline Validated Architectural Design Reviews. The quality output has been the result of the dedication of TSA and CISA staff, in partnership with pipeline operators, toward a shared common goal—pipeline security."[2]

This level of collaboration should be the model as TSA, in partnership with CISA, works to develop the aviation and rail directives. Industry has a level of expertise that will be essential in understanding what needs to be done. Businesses rarely embrace Government mandates; that is not surprising. Nevertheless, industry must be at the table to help craft directives that are ambitious but achievable, and Government must invite them early enough in the process to allow to make a meaningful contribution.

It's also important to note that the security directive process allows the TSA administrator flexibility to work with businesses even after the directive is issued. For example, a company can propose alternative measures for achieving the objective(s), and the administrator can amend or issue new directives as conditions warrant.

DHS has indicated that these temporary directives will be replaced with regulations, presumably no later than 1 year from their issuance, when they are set to expire. The informal consultation with industry will, pursuant to the Administrative Procedures Act, be supplemented by a formal notice and comment process. Not only should the industries directly covered by the proposed regulations weigh in, those who depend upon these critical sectors should also let their voices be heard as the Government considers how best to ensure the security, safety, and reliability of these critical functions in the face of growing cyber risks. In addition, these regulations should be informed by an awareness of the tools and technologies that are available to help these asset owners and operators gain visibility into their information technology (IT) and operational technology (OT) systems, detect malicious activity, and respond quickly and effectively. To encourage continued innovation in this area, Government should lean toward open, performance-based standards that are technology-neutral and vendor-agnostic.

Furthermore, any new regulations should draw on existing guidelines, standards, and best practices. They should be harmonized with requirements in other sectors, particularly as between the pipeline and electric sectors, in which there is often significant overlap.

---

[2] https://homeland.house.gov/imo/media/doc/2021-09-01-CIPI-HRG-Testimony-Denbow.pdf.

Finally, TSA has been working to build its cyber capacity, but it should not try to duplicate expertise that resides at CISA. These two DHS entities should continue to work closely together, with TSA bringing industry relationships and expertise together with CISA's cyber-specific and critical infrastructure resilience expertise. The work of the National Risk Management Center should inform the identification of highest-risk/highest-consequence functions. Congress needs to ensure that DHS is provided the resources necessary to effectively implement these mandates and to continue its equally important voluntary work with these vital industries.

Time is not on our side. The threat environment grows more dangerous with each passing day. In the recent words of one administration official, "the overall environment is more aggressive; more sophisticated; and more belligerent . . . "[3]

The general assessment is that neither state nor non-state actors have current intent to cause significant disruption. But cyber incidents can have unintended consequences. NotPetya came back to impact Russian companies. And if we are to believe the criminals involved in the Colonial Pipeline attack, they did not intend to disrupt pipeline operations. I am inclined to believe that, since it would've been hard to predict that an intrusion into the corporate IT system, as opposed to the OT system, would have such a significant impact on operations. It is a reminder that lack of intent should not give us great comfort.

Moreover, intent can change. Even short of a direct kinetic conflict in which an adversary might decide to disrupt our critical infrastructure, there is the prospect of an adversary using the credible threat of such disruption to deter us from taking actions in our National interest. Having this leverage could embolden China in the South China Sea or Russia in Ukraine or elsewhere, for example. It seems likely that Russia's cyberattacks on Ukraine's electric grid were designed not only to undermine the Ukraine government but to send a signal to the United States about Russia's capabilities.

Perhaps most troubling is the threat of a destructive attack on the safety systems of operations, leading not just to disruption but to potentially catastrophic deadly consequences. In 2017, a Saudi petrochemical plant was hit with malware later dubbed "Triton" which disabled the Safety Instrumented System (SIS). SISs are the last line of automated safety defense for industrial facilities, designed to prevent equipment failure and catastrophic

---

[3] https://www.justice.gov/opa/speech/deputy-attorney-general-lisa-o-monaco-and-assistant-attorney-general-kenneth-polite-jr.

incidents such as explosions or fire. Faulty code prevented that attack from succeeding but experts say the technique is replicable by others. Moreover, in 2019, the attackers behind the Triton malware, attributed to a Russian government-funded research institution, were reported to be scanning and probing at least 20 electric utilities in the United States for vulnerabilities.

The bipartisan co-chairs of the Solarium have noted that it was envisioned as a 9/11 commission to avert a cyber 9/11. We should not wait for a tragedy caused by malicious cyber activity in one of these vital sectors before we take the necessary action. The proposed TSA directives reflect a growing body of evidence that the risk of serious disruptions to critical infrastructure is not "potential" or in the future, it is here now and requires an urgent response.

Thank you and I look forward to your questions.

Ms. CLARKE. We thank you for your testimony, Ms. Spaulding.

I now recognize Ms. Cogswell to summarize her statement for 5 minutes.

Statement of Patricia F.S. Cogswell, Strategic Advisor, Guidehouse; Former Deputy Administrator, Transportation Security Administration

Ms. COGSWELL. Chairwoman Clarke, Chairwoman Watson Coleman, Ranking Member Garbarino, and Ranking Member Gimenez, and the distinguished Members of the subcommittees, thank you for the opportunity to testify before you this afternoon on transportation:

The insights I will share today are informed by my 24 years of Federal service, serving in varied capacities from the founding of DHS through my retirement as the deputy administrator of the Transportation Security Administration.

My first significant engagement in countering cybersecurity threats to industrial control systems was while I served as the special assistant to the President for Transborder Security at the National Security Council after the 2012 cyberattack on Saudi Aramco.

Since that time, I have seen the number of security threats increase, with an expanding number and type of threat actors, including both state and non-state actors such as transnational criminal entities; an increased focus by them on exploiting network-connected ICS vulnerabilities; and an increasing level of risk faced across our transportation infrastructure for both the combination of increased threat but also of consequence as we see how an attack on one entity can affect the entire sector.

I have also seen very strong partnerships across Government and industry to develop tools, programs, information-sharing mechanisms, and standards to mitigate the risks, including the NIST framework, TSA's pipeline security guidelines, and various multientity exercises.

I am pleased to be able to be here today and hope that I can assist you as you consider how best Congress can support and enable transportation cybersecurity.

I thank you for your willingness to call attention to this incredibly important topic. I want to recognize the work that this committee, along with Senate Homeland Security and Government Affairs and the Defense Armed Services Committee, are leading to promote and standardize cyber incident reporting.

As this committee further examines roles, responsibilities, and activities, I would highlight the following: First is the value of TSA's authority to issue security directives. Security directives have repeatedly demonstrated their value, providing a mechanism for TSA and industry to put immediate protective mitigation measures in place. They send a clear message to our adversaries, to the American people, and to our allies.

After the recent pipeline ransomware event, TSA security directives were the tool of choice. SDs are most effective, as you have noted, when TSA and the regulated industry are able to work together throughout the entire process from development of requirement through implementation.

Second, promote bidirectional partnership through analysis of reporting data. As I have spoken with industry and Government about the new cyber requirements, several colleagues expressed their interest in using this reporting to promote a deeper understanding of and engagement around cyber threats to critical infrastructure. There is a recognition that analyzing the threats of vulnerabilities associated with industrial control systems can tell us more about the prevalence and use of tactics, the effectiveness of measures to counter those tactics, and best practices to follow. Continued investment in open standards development. NIST and DHS, through CISA and TSA, have established cybersecurity and standards environments for ICS and critical infrastructure. Continued evolution that provides transportation owners and operators with an opportunity to participate in that development and a mechanism to communicate direction to solutions developers and providers should be encouraged.

Finally, incentivizing and encouraging innovative approaches, while requiring transportation operators to achieve minimum standards. As DHS looks to advance regulatory requirements for transportation operators, I anticipate it will look to adopt a set of baseline requirements based on current best practices and recommendations, with the aim of continuing to update them over time. DHS and Congress should consider innovative mechanisms for how to achieve these goals, using a model that emphasizes performance-based outcomes and allows industry to use alternative methods to reach compliance.

This can be further encouraged through a regulatory model where transportation operators can use a qualified third party to complete the cybersecurity architecture reviews or planning required, similar to TSA's third-party canine program, and providing operators with access to a list of qualified entities who can provide such functions and services, such as GSA does for identity management and credentials, or providing other recognized criteria.

Cybersecurity, it is often said, is a team sport. Having many players on the field with standards-based interoperable solutions will enable innovation and enhance the protection of our critical infrastructure.

As you consider statutory language, I would encourage you to develop it in a way that will create an enduring framework that supports the evolution of cybersecurity as the threats and risks continue to change. A technology-neutral approach based on open standards that promote competition, innovation, and interoperability should be the core of such effort.

Thank you again for the opportunity to testify before you today. I look forward to your questions.

[The prepared statement of Ms. Cogswell follows:]

Testimony of Patricia F.S. Cogswell Senior Strategic Advisor for National Security Guidehouse

Chairman Thompson, Ranking Member Katko, and distinguished Members of the subcommittees, thank you for the opportunity to testify before you this morning on Transportation Cybersecurity.

The insights I will share with the committee today are informed by my 24 years of Federal service, my long-standing tenure as a founding member of DHS serving on Day 1, and the varied capacities in which I have served the transportation security mission of DHS through my retirement as deputy administrator for the Transportation Security Administration.

My first significant engagement in countering cybersecurity threats to industrial control systems (ICS) was while I served as special assistant to the President for transborder security, at the National Security Council after the 2012 cyberattack on Saudi Aramco.

Since that time, I've seen:

- The number of cyber threats increase—with an expanding number and type of threat actors, including both state and non-state actors, including transnational criminal entities;
- Targeted exploitation of vulnerabilities in ICS-environment management practices;
- An increased recognition of the risk faced across our critical transportation infrastructure, from the combination of threat, vulnerability, and consequence; and
- Partnership across Government and industry to develop tools, programs, information-sharing mechanisms, and standards to mitigate the risk, including the NIST Framework for Improving Critical Infrastructure Security, TSA's Pipeline Security Guidelines, and various multentity exercises, such as 2020 Ohio Cyber shield.

I am pleased to be here today to speak before the committee, and hope that I can assist you as you consider how Congress can best support and enable critical infrastructure cybersecurity. I thank you for your willingness to call attention to this very important topic. I also want to recognize the legislation this committee, along with Senate Homeland Security and Government Affairs, and the Defense Armed Services Committee are leading to promote and standardize cyber incident reporting to DHS's Cybersecurity and Critical Infrastructure Agency (CISA).

As this committee further examines how to incentivize the right mix of roles, responsibilities, and activities across Government and industry, I'd highlight the following areas as important in our common interest in making progress:

- The value of TSA's authority to issue Security Directives. SDs have repeatedly demonstrated their value, providing a mechanism for TSA and industry, often in concert with DOT and other Federal entities, to put immediate measures into place—and sending a clear message to our adversaries, to the American people, and to our allies. After the recent pipeline ransomware event, there was an understandable interest across the administration, Congress, industry, and the public in taking action. TSA's authority to issue Security Directives for the transportation industry in response to emerging threats was the tool of choice to rapidly direct owners and operators of pipeline and natural gas facilities to implement necessary cyber protections. TSA's SDs are most effective when TSA and the regulated industries work together throughout the process to ensure that requirements are achievable under the time lines set and the regulated industries, all the way down the individual companies can work through implementation.

- Promote bidirectional partnership through analysis of reporting data. As I've spoken with individuals in industry and Government about the new CISA cybersecurity reporting requirements, several colleagues expressed their interest in using this to promote a deeper understanding and engagement of cyber threats to critical infrastructure, particularly where they can be done in a Classified setting. While there are significant differences in transportation modes of operation, there is a recognition that analyzing the threats and vulnerabilities associated with industrial control systems across critical infrastructure sectors can tell us more about the prevalence and use of adversaries' tactics, the effectiveness of measures to counter those tactics, and best practices to follow. That analysis is also critical to feed back to the industries required to report cyber incidents to provide them with that deeper understanding of the threats and vulnerabilities to proactively assess additional areas of focus for their own systems and operations. These should then be considered for adoption and reinforcement through regulatory programs.
- Invest in continued evolution of open standards. NIST and DHS, through both CISA and TSA, along with other agencies, have established a cyber standards environment for ICS and critical infrastructure. This environment provides transportation owners and operators with insight and visibility, as well as the opportunity to participate in standards development. It also creates a mechanism to communicate direction to solutions developers and providers.

- Incentivize and encourage innovative approaches, while requiring transportation operators to achieve minimum standards. Consistent with our approach to other transportation security issues, DHS should look to advance regulatory requirements for transportation operators. These could be a formalization of actions already encouraged now or recognized industry best practices, such as the validated architecture reviews, with the aim of changing over time as the standards evolve. By setting these baseline requirements, we can ensure that critical infrastructure operators are on an even playing field, and that the industry as a whole is less vulnerable to the actions of a small few.

The Government should also consider innovative mechanisms for how to achieve these goals, using a model that emphasizes performance-based outcomes, and allows industry to use alternative methods to reach compliance. A more open model also addresses the issues associated with vendor lock or over reliance on a single set of tools, which can disincentivize innovation. Cybersecurity, it's often said, is a team sport. Having as many players on the field with standards-based solutions interoperable solutions will enable innovation and enhance the protection of our critical infrastructure.

I would also encourage DHS to establish a regulatory environment where a transportation operator can use a qualified third-party entity to complete the cybersecurity architecture reviews or planning required. From a statutory and regulatory perspective, this could look similar to how TSA established the third-party canine program. This type of model would increase speed of adoption, and provide transportation operators options for meeting the requirements. But, from industry colleagues I have talked to, transportation operators must have access to a list of Government-approved third-party entities, or be able to rely on firms that meet specified criteria. My understanding is that the pipeline industry is already working to begin to identify those criteria and identifying firms who could serve these needs. To scale this model effectively given the number of critical infrastructure entities, both public and private, that would benefit from industrial control systems cybersecurity expertise, it may make sense to look to GSA to manage the vendor qualification process, with DHS and other entities contributing their expertise, similar to other cross-cutting needs.

As you consider statutory language, I would encourage you to develop it in a way that will create an enduring framework that supports the evolution of cybersecurity as the threats and risks continue to change. A technology-neutral approach based on open standards that promote competition, innovation, and interoperability should be the core of any such effort.

Thank you again for the opportunity to testify before you today. I look forward to your questions.

Ms. CLARKE. Thank you, Ms. Cogswell, for your testimony.

Members should know that votes have been called, but we will continue to receive testimony from our final two witnesses today. So I now recognize Mr. Troy to summarize his statement for 5 minutes.

Statement of Jeffrey L. Troy, President, CEO, Aviation Information Sharing and Analysis Center; Former Deputy Assistant Director, Cyber Division, Federal Bureau of Investigation

Mr. TROY. Thank you, Chairwoman, Chairwoman, and Ranking Members, and Members of the committee.

Good afternoon. My name is Jeffrey Troy. I am president of the Aviation Information Sharing and Analysis Center.

The Aviation ISAC is a global nonprofit. Our members are on 5 continents and include air framers, airlines, airports, air navigation service providers, and more. Our mission is to make the aviation industry more resilient to cyberattacks.

Last time I came before you was in September 2018, and thank you for the opportunity to talk to you once again about the cyber risk landscape in aviation.

The cyber risks to the aviation industry have increased. Together, both private industry and the public sector have significantly increased cooperation and threat intelligence and best practices sharing, and now is the time for industry and Government to partner even more closely in creating and enhancing effective cyber risk reduction frameworks.

Over the past several years, ransomware has become a common term in aviation and many other sectors. The success of ransomware operators to extort money from their victims has greatly increased the level of skill and the number of persons willing to conduct ransomware attacks. The second-stage ransomware events, wherein additional ransoms are sought in exchange for deletion of sensitive records stolen as a part of the ransom operation, also highlights the risk, the theft of intellectual property, sensitive business information, and privacy data.

Ransomware can also shut down operations. This has the potential to be very impactful to the aviation industry. Pardon me. Ransomware—excuse me—it also becomes more complicated in the aviation industry because many of the operational technologies are mobile. The attack on Colonial Pipeline, which has been spoken of today, and the QNX real-time operating system vulnerability are two examples of where a cyberattack or a vulnerability in a product can have a ripple effect across many sectors.

Preventing, responding to, and limiting the impact of these attacks requires a team-of-teams approach. Our core values include creating and maintaining partnerships with numerous Government and private-sector entities. The Aviation ISAC is proud to have partnered with the Aviation Cyber Initiative, a joint partnership led by DOD, FAA, and the DHS, which is in the process of transferring this trichair seat to the TSA.

This year, the Aviation ISAC and the ACI significantly solidified our partnership by co-hosting a summit on aviation cybersecurity. We are also proud to partner with CISA. CISA is maturing well and has been put out timely, relevant guidance in direct response to recent cyberattacks on critical infrastructure and the supply chain. On 6 occasions our intelligence was used in CISA's intelligence bulletins and intelligence information reports.

Similarly, we have reached out to the TSA as they build their cybersecurity strategy and create a regulatory framework over cyber events in aviation. Our industry is also benefiting from a significant increase in cooperation between private entities. This includes the Aerospace Village, the Aerospace Industries Association, the American Institute of Aeronautics and Astronautics, along with Airlines for America.

The Aviation ISAC is also working with ICAO, the United Nations group—excuse me—International Civil Aviation Organization, and working with them on their aviation cybersecurity strategy and their cybersecurity action plan. We are also working several other initiatives, to include secure interoperability strategies across the globe.

As the United States considers legislation such as mandatory cyber reporting, the Aviation ISAC has been reaching out to educate stakeholders to ensure that the regulatory requirements are risk-based, achievable, cost-effective, and do not degrade the success the private sector has had in reducing cyber risks through ISACs like ours.

With respect to the mandatory reporting requirements, we believe it is important that the mandatory reporting is scoped to well-defined and confirmed cyber incidents, that mandatory reporting requirements should include robust liability protections, and it is critical that Congress streamlines the Federal and State reporting requirements to ensure that industry resources are used efficiently to combat malicious cyber threats rather than customizing reports on the same incident for multiple agencies. We also believe that the reporting program should encourage cooperation and strengthen trust between the public and private sectors, which would include bidirectional information sharing.

Information reported to the Government needs to be properly aggregated, anonymized, analyzed, and shared with industry to help prevent future incidents.

Thank you again for the opportunity to come before you today and work on this important matter with cybersecurity and aviation.

[The prepared statement of Mr. Troy follows:]

Prepared Statement of Jeffrey L. Troy

Good afternoon. My name is Jeffrey Troy. I am the president of the Aviation Information Sharing and Analysis Center or Aviation ISAC. The Aviation ISAC is a global non-profit. Our members are on five continents and include air framers, airlines, airports, air navigation service providers, satellite companies, and more. Our mission is to make the aviation industry more resilient to cyberattacks.

The last time I came before you was in September 2018. Thank you for this opportunity to talk with you once again about the changes to the cyber risk landscape in aviation. The cyber risks to the aviation industry have increased. I will share with you about the good work being done by both the public and private sectors. Together both private industry and the public sector have significantly increased cooperation in threat intelligence and best practices sharing. Now is the time for industry and Government to partner even more closely in creating and enhancing effective cyber risk reduction frameworks.

Increase in Threat Actor Activity

Over the past several years ransomware has become a common term in aviation and many other sectors. A breach is a breach, but the success of ransomware extortionists to collect money from their victims, has greatly increased the level of skill and the number of persons willing to conduct cyberattacks. Second stage ransomware events, wherein additional ransoms are sought in exchange for the deletion of sensitive records stolen as a part of the ransom operation also highlights the risk to theft of intellectual property, sensitive business information, and privacy data.

Ransomware can also shut down operations. This has the potential to be very impactful on the aviation industry as the aviation ecosystem is supported by many operational technologies.

Other cyber and cyber-related activity include business email compromises, ransom in lieu of a Distributed Denial of Service (DDoS) attack, and other frauds.

These attacks are both directly on segments of the aviation industry such as air framers, airlines, airports, etc., and their supply chains. The attack on the Colonial Pipeline and QNX Real Time Operating System (RTOS) vulnerability are two examples of where a cyberattack or a vulnerability in a product can have a ripple effect across many sectors.

Increased Collaboration

The aviation industry is a unique, global ecosystem. Much of our critical infrastructure is mobile. Each industry segment, air framers, airlines, airports, services and more, are dependent on each other effectively monitoring and responding to their cyber risk. In the same way, as our assets move around the world, we benefit from trusted, global cooperation and intelligence sharing.

Preventing, responding to, and limiting the impact of these attacks requires a team of teams approach. The Aviation ISAC is primarily private-sector members. However, our core values include creating and maintaining partnerships with numerous Government and private-sector entities.

We are working with many Government agencies to make the industry more resilient by identifying and reducing cyber risks. The Aviation Cyber Initiative (ACI) is a joint partnership with the Department of Defense (DOD), the Federal Aviation Administration (FAA) and the Department of Homeland Security (DHS) which is in the process of transferring this tri-chair seat to the

Transportation Security Administration (TSA). This year the Aviation ISAC and the ACI significantly solidified our partnership by co-hosting a Summit on Aviation Cybersecurity. This 3-day event included domestic and international leaders and cybersecurity experts from both the Government and private sector.

We are proud to partner with DHS's Cybersecurity and Infrastructure Security Agency (CISA). CISA is maturing well and has been putting out timely, relevant guidance in direct response to recent cyberattacks on critical infrastructure and the supply chain. The Aviation ISAC has shared intelligence on 18 occasions which were used in part in six of CISAs Intelligence Bulletins and Intelligence Information Reports. CISA has also been reaching out on vulnerability disclosures. It is also promising to learn the TSA is considering CISA as an agent for the collection of soon-to-be-required mandatory reporting of cyber events impacting aviation.

Similarly, we have reached out to the TSA as they build their cybersecurity strategy and create a regulatory framework over cyber events in Aviation.

The Aviation ISAC has been in the forefront of ringing the bell on the ransomware problem. We have been a strong voice in the crowd calling for action to reduce and eliminate this threat. We were honored to be a part of a group represented by the Government and private sector in the writing of the "Combatting Ransomware Report" issued in late April by the Institute for Security and Technology. The report has many actionable recommendations. The world needs a stronger international consensus on identifying ransomware operators and taking them out of action. Law enforcement efforts must be enhanced with private-sector expertise and a whole-of-Government as well as a whole-of-governments working together. We encourage continued action on the recommendations in this report.

Aviation is global. The Aviation ISAC has members on five continents and from many segments of the Aviation industry. We engage with global Computer Emergency Response Teams, the International Civil Aviation Organization (ICAO), International Air Transport Association (IATA), Airports Council International, and many European Union entities, to name a few.

The public-private partnerships still have a long way to go, especially in the area of trust, which I will talk about in a few minutes. Our industry is also benefiting from a significant increase in the cooperation between "Private-Private" entities.

To highlight a few, the Aviation ISAC has partnered with the Aerospace Village. Each year, we sponsor a cyber skills event, also known as a capture the flag event. The Aerospace Village has many cybersecurity researchers as members. This is a great event for building bridges between industry and the researcher community.

We partner with the Aerospace Industries Association, contributing to discussions and development of a white paper on best practices in aviation cybersecurity.

We also partner with the American Institute of Aeronautics and Astronautics (AIAA) and have a regular dialog with Airlines for America.

The Aviation ISAC and our members are also building bridges with security researchers through the creation, promotion, and ease of access to Vulnerability Disclosure programs. These programs make manufacturers more accessible to security researchers who can make vulnerabilities known to manufacturers of software and hardware products.

Creating and Enhancing Effective Risk Reduction Frameworks

There are many efforts going on across the globe to increase the regulatory requirements related to cybersecurity in Aviation. Earlier I mentioned ICAO, a United Nations organization, which establishes guidance for the aviation industry around the world. The Aviation ISAC is working with ICAO and partners across the globe in updating ICAO's Aviation Cybersecurity Action Plan. We are also working on several other initiatives to include an aviation cybersecurity framework and secure interoperability strategies.

As the U.S. Government considers legislation such as mandatory cyber reporting, the Aviation ISAC has been reaching out to educate aviation stakeholders to ensure that the regulatory requirements are risk-based, achievable, cost-effective, and do not degrade the success the private sector has had in reducing cyber risk through ISACs like ours.

Regarding Mandatory Reporting Requirements

1. We believe it is important that mandatory reporting is scoped to well-defined and -confirmed cyber incidents. We must be focused on quality information sharing. Too much information will overload threat intelligence and incident response resources.

2. Any mandatory reporting requirements should include robust liability protections. The act of reporting a covered incident and the contents of any report, including supplemental reporting, should be protected from legal liability. Information contained in notifications should not be subject to discovery in any civil or criminal action. Reporting entities, in essence, should not be penalized after the fact for complying with a legal obligation. In addition, only relevant information which will assist others in protecting and defending critical infrastructure systems should be required of the sector regulator.
3. Several critical infrastructure sectors have existing obligations to report significant cyber incidents to Federal and/or State regulatory agencies. It is crucial that Congress streamlines Federal and State reporting requirements to ensure that industry resources are used efficiently to combat malicious cyber threats, rather than customizing reports on the same incident for multiple agencies. A single report to one agency should suffice to meet legislative and regulatory mandates. For example, many aviation sector companies are also defense contractors. Reporting should be made either to CISA or the appropriate sector risk management agency (SRMA), which should then disseminate reports to other relevant agencies.
4. Cyberattack victims are victims. A reporting program should encourage cooperation and strengthen trust between the public and private sectors. A regulatory-based approach that focuses on punitive actions, such as fines or penalties, rather than mutual gains achieved through information sharing runs counter to the goal of creating a strong National partnership model to address the increasing cyber threats facing the United States.
5. The bills in draft would require CISA to take the lead in writing an interim final rule. Lawmakers are urged to step back from this line of thinking and call on CISA to first provide notice that it intends to promulgate a rule. With input from industry, the process will work faster as industry can assist in making the rules achievable. Industry is passionate about protecting our customers, employees, and our businesses. We are operators of critical infrastructure and our industry has incredible passion and cybersecurity talent working to protect it. The rule-making process must include coordination with impacted private industry stakeholders because many of the programmatic details, such as definitions and the contents of reporting, would be

determined through the rulemaking process. At a minimum, we ask you to consider a rulemaking process which features an initial 90-day consultation period with industry followed by a 90-day comment period.
6. Cyber intelligence is a requirement to protect the sector. It is not a singular need of the Government, nor the private sector. Information reported to Government needs to be promptly aggregated, anonymized, analyzed, and shared with industry to foster the mitigation and/or prevention of future cyber incidents. Nothing in future legislation or processes should limit or impede companies continuing to work together through ISACs. With respect to the Government sharing back information to the private sector, in many cases, the private sector will be able to enhance that information, keeping the intelligence cycle active and benefiting us all as we protect aviation. A persistent shortcoming experienced by businesses across many sectors is a lack of timely and effective action or feedback on cyber reports from Government. We need legislation that leads CISA, law enforcement, and other agencies to provide more timely, relevant cyber intelligence to industry groups' and sector businesses.

Conclusion

We have made great strides in coming together as a Government and an industry in making aviation more resilient to cyberattacks. We applaud the efforts of the Government to continue to strengthen the ability of our Government entities to investigate, prosecute, and dismantle ransomware gangs. We will continue to partner and engage with the Aviation Cyber Initiative and our many partners as we seek out vulnerabilities and develop best practices to protect, defend, respond to, and mitigate cyberattacks. We applaud the efforts of CISA in publishing vulnerability and best practices and encourage more bidirectional information sharing. Finally, thank you once again for the opportunity to come before you today on this important matter of cybersecurity in aviation.

Ms. CLARKE. Thank you, Mr. Troy, for your testimony.

I now recognize Mr. Dickinson—Mr. Dickerson—excuse me—to summarize his statement for 5 minutes.

Statement of Scott Dickerson, Executive Director, Maritime Transportation System Information Sharing and Analysis Center

Mr. DICKERSON. Thank you, Chairwomen, Ranking Members, and Members of the subcommittees. My name is Scott Dickerson, and I serve as the executive director of the nonprofit Maritime Transportation System Information Sharing and Analysis Center, the MTS–ISAC. A decade ago, helped create the Coast Guard Cyber Command, before serving in other civilian roles and supporting private-sector cybersecurity programs. Thank you for the opportunity to testify before the subcommittees today.

The MTS–ISAC is made up of public and private-sector stakeholders, including port authorities, vessel and terminal owners and operators, cruise lines, energy facilities, ferry operators, and other members of the maritime community. We focus on actionable, relevant, and timely cyber threat information sharing. We have supported cybersecurity guidelines on-board vessels, as well as cybersecurity guidelines for ports and port facilities, both of which are recognized by the U.N.'s International Maritime Organization.

Our efforts have resulted in significantly more cybersecurity advisories being distributed to our maritime community than those released by the 20-plus Federal Government organizations with the responsibility for maritime security combined. A key reason for the level of sharing we see is the anonymization of identities and the trust that this reinforces with the maritime community. Others may tell you we need billions of dollars in cybersecurity investment across the critical infrastructure sectors. We do need investment, but taxpayers may currently be overpaying for the results the critical infrastructure community is receiving from the Federal Government.

I want to share with you three common challenges I regularly hear from industry stakeholders related to the Federal Government's approach to cybersecurity and public-private partnership. First is the concern of redundant Federal cybersecurity efforts. Because of the critical intermodal connections that ports, terminals, and a variety of facilities have, some of our stakeholders are subject to multiple regulatory requirements, including the Maritime Transportation Security Act of 2002, as well as TSA's pipeline and soon-to-be-finalized rail security directives.

As a result, limited resources are often spent on redundant checklists, meetings, reports, audits, et cetera, as opposed to actively managing cyber risks to critical infrastructure. It seems like every time we turn around, there is a new effort unveiled by a government agency, and often it seems to be repackaging the elements of an older program with a new name. The latest example is JCDC, elements of which have been in place for several years.

Second, there is a lack of trust with the Federal Government related to cyber incident reporting. Trust is critical when fostering collaboration and information sharing. The maritime community's trust in Federal agencies was yet again recently shaken in the aftermath of an incident at a port. This is because of three things. No. 1, immediately following the incident, the 3 Federal Government agencies involved did not want industry-sharing actionable information for almost 3 weeks as zero-day vulnerabilities were actively being exploited. Of note, during this 3-week period, none of those agencies collaborated with the MTS–ISAC or the maritime industry writ large.

No. 2, CISA publicly released the name of the victim, with no prior coordination or notice to the victim. This may have been in violation of the Cybersecurity Information Sharing Act of 2015 and undermine trust.

No. 3, a government agency for-official-use-only technical report with details surrounding the incident was leaked to the press, but it was not shared amongst maritime community members.

These were 3 distinct ways industry trust was undermined with just this one incident, and, unfortunately, incidents are occurring regularly.

Third, resource investments in people are needed. Experienced cybersecurity specialists are in short supply in all industries. Please review opportunities for partnering with ISACs for real-world hands-on cybersecurity training, internships, and educational opportunities. Also, Federal employees need to better understand the various cybersecurity funding opportunities the Government provides to align with their agency mission sets.

As an example, cybersecurity was the highest-stated priority for FEMA's 2020 Port Security Grant Program. Yet many stakeholder requests for cybersecurity investments were turned down by U.S. Coast Guard captains of the port, resulting in only about 12 percent of the $100 million program being invested in cybersecurity, the No. 1 priority.

MTS–ISAC and the stakeholders are hopeful that we can more effectively partner with the Federal Government to safeguard our national interests. I kindly request you include, support, and protect the mechanisms safeguarding trusted, anonymous information sharing, incident reporting, and other critical infrastructure cybersecurity efforts performed by ISACs and their communities in legislation.

Of note, CISA of 2015 remains significantly underutilized. Although it has been implemented, there remains resistance to fully trusting and using the provisions of the legislation. Perhaps we should focus on some of these underutilized efforts rather than creating some new ones.

Thank you again for the opportunity to provide this testimony, and I look forward to your questions.

[The prepared statement of Mr. Dickerson follows:]

Prepared Statement of Scott Dickerson

I. Background

Ranking Member Garbarino, Ranking Member Gimenez, and Members of the subcommittee: My name is Scott Dickerson and I serve as the executive director of the Maritime Transportation System Information Sharing and Analysis Center Institute (MTS–ISAC). Thank you for the opportunity to testify before the committee today. The Maritime Transportation System ISAC was formed as a nonprofit by a group of U.S. maritime critical infrastructure stakeholders. Our primary mission is to more effectively share information focused on cyber threats and cybersecurity best practices within a trusted community of stakeholders to help make the maritime community more resilient to cyberattacks. Our stakeholders include port authorities, vessel owners and operators, terminal owners and operators, cruise lines, energy facilities, ferry operators, and other members of the public and private-sector maritime critical infrastructure community. On a daily basis, our stakeholders are sharing actionable, timely, and relevant cyber threat information with their public and private-sector peers. They formed the MTS–ISAC out of a need to quickly share relevant cyber threat information and have quickly shown how effective their ISAC model is working to do just that.

MTS–ISAC stakeholders exchange information every day about the attacks they are seeing. The MTS–ISAC provides anonymization of identities, which when combined with the Cybersecurity Information Sharing Act of 2015 (CISA 2015), fosters community trust and enables peer-to-peer collaboration. This peer-to-peer collaboration is extremely valuable because it allows stakeholders to better understand threats targeting the maritime sector and implement cybersecurity strategies more effectively to counter those attacks. This private-sector sharing has resulted in more maritime industry-focused cyber threat intelligence advisories being distributed to our stakeholders since our inception than those released by the more than 20

Federal Government organizations with a responsibility for maritime security[4] combined. As an example, we have produced over 80 Cybersecurity Advisories this year and to our knowledge the U.S. Coast Guard has released 5 cybersecurity threat reports. The MTS–ISAC has not received any cyber threat or incident reporting from MARAD, Department of Energy, TSA, USTRANSCOM, NOAA, ODNI's National Maritime Intelligence-Integration Office (NMIO), and or other maritime-focused Governmental organizations. We have created over 500 Indicator Bulletins sourced from stakeholder shares, which I believe is roughly on par with the whole of CISA. We do this on a nonprofit budget that runs in the low 6 figures annually.

Our stakeholders believe that cybersecurity is a core element of risk management that allows their organizations to operate in a safe and secure manner. Because of the critical intermodal connections and relationships that ports, terminals, and a variety of facilities have, some of our stakeholders are subject to a variety of regulations and security directives, including the Maritime Transportation Security Act of 2002 as well as TSA's Pipeline and soon to be finalized Rail Security Directives. This is in addition to a variety of other cybersecurity-related requirements that can include safeguarding various types of information including HIPAA, PCI, PII, and other cybersecurity frameworks and requirements. I say this not to be glib, but to say the maritime sector faces a highly complex intersection of requirements, and maritime companies understand how to operate in this environment. Cyber incidents need to be handled extremely delicately since they can have major impact across supply chains, for customers, stakeholders, and shareholders. Legal departments and auditors within an organization help work these details in closed door sessions to ensure compliance and legal issues are addressed properly. Additionally, those with cyber insurance coverage will be directed by their insurance how and with whom to share information. It would be beneficial for the Federal Government to consult with stakeholders before new cybersecurity laws, security directives, or similar facets of oversight are finalized to fully understand the implications of drafts so that the desired risk management outcomes can be met in a manner appropriate for the complexities of this industry without creating undue burdens or unintended consequences.

In addition to sharing cyber threat information, our nonprofit is also working with numerous industry stakeholders to improve industry cybersecurity guidelines. We have provided inputs to drafts for updates to the

---

[4] National Maritime Cybersecurity Plan—https://www.hsdl.org/?abstract&did=848704.

International Association of Classification Societies' Recommendations on Cyber Resilience. The MTS–ISAC also contributed content to the following maritime industry cybersecurity references:

- The Guidelines on Cybersecurity Onboard Ships (V4) and
- IAPH Cybersecurity Guidelines for Ports and Port Facilities (Version 1.0).

II. Current Challenges with Federal Cybersecurity Approaches

There are currently multiple cybersecurity challenges impacting critical infrastructure cyber resiliency. Of particular interest from an ISAC perspective are the following:

Overlapping Efforts

- Redundant, and sometimes conflicting cyber regulations and enforcement or interpretation differences across Government roles and responsibilities.
- Multiple agencies are involved with duplicative efforts. Redundant tracking, outreach, reporting, and mitigation efforts are a detriment to securing critical infrastructure as the time of limited resources is spent on redundant efforts.
- Inconsistent standards often impact multiple sectors and cause confusion.
- Federal Government focus on "leading," rather than partnering to support private-sector efforts. The private sector predominantly owns and operates critical infrastructure, and the Federal Government should support effective solutions rather than lead ineffective solutions.
- Private sector understands where the challenges lie; multiple Governmental agencies try to "solve the problem" in silos rather than in partnership.

Information and Intelligence Sharing

- There is currently a Federal Government focus on cyber incident reporting, rather than exchanging timely threat information that could minimize potential impacts.
- Lack of consistent and clear definitions for suspicious activity, incidents, etc.—this needs to be remedied and should be in partnership with industry.
- CISA should be the Federal agency hub for information sharing, and that needs to be reflected in all regulations, Security Directives, etc. Having a single touchpoint will streamline processes and should allow for more cross-sector critical infrastructure correlations to be made that are currently being missed.
- Similarly, there are concerns with USCG being both a regulator and pushing for threat intel sharing outside of the required reporting mandates. Providing non-mandatory event reporting to a regulator is a cause for concern for some in the private sector. This should be voluntary (and based on trust), but again it would be better to have a single point of contact for all critical infrastructure sector reporting, which for maritime can then be provided to the 20+ Federal Government organizations with a responsibility for maritime security.
- Repeated misinformation that private sector does not share information with each other or with Governmental agencies.
- Greater Federal resource emphasis on granting security clearances to private-sector stakeholders, who remain constrained on acting on Classified information.
- Agency and media inaccurate claims that certain sectors are better or worse in cybersecurity protections pit private industry as competitors, not collaborators.

Cybersecurity Resourcing

- Experienced cybersecurity specialists are in short supply in all sectors and across the public and private sectors.
- Federal funding of cybersecurity efforts remains inconsistent across sectors and sometimes competes with private-sector cybersecurity efforts, which confuses and frustrates maritime stakeholders.

In addition to these, there are numerous other cybersecurity challenges that also need addressing, but others that are notable include:

- Risks related to foreign investment and/or reliance within U.S. marine critical infrastructure;
- A heavy focus on check-box style types of regulation;
- Recent TSA Pipeline Security Directive did not include a mechanism for review and feedback from the stakeholders this will impact. As a result, some challenges may be arising that could have been avoided if some language was changed. For example, requiring to inform the Government within 7 days of personnel that will be designated to be available 24/7 to the Government for any reason. There are several H.R. implications for this, including the potential need to reclassify positions, renegotiate contracts, etc. for the personnel in those roles; and
- Lack of funding for voluntary CISA cybersecurity programs, including CISA Risk and Vulnerability Assessments (RVA), Validated Architecture Design Reviews (VADR), and similar efforts within the Coast Guard, such as their outstanding Cyber Protection Team.

III. Recent Example of Post-Incident Response

A recent incident at a critical port is an example of a post incident response that highlights some of the above challenges and how the Federal Government is currently handling critical infrastructure cybersecurity.

Summary
A port quickly identified and responded to a cyberattack exploiting a zero-day vulnerability. The port confirmed the incident with their security vendor, who was able to identify other clients in other critical infrastructure sectors also experiencing the same attack. The port notified CISA, USCG, FBI and MTS–ISAC. The MTS– ISAC shared information with stakeholders and with other members of the National Council of ISACs the same day.

The Federal agencies worked with the vendor on a patch but stated they did not want vulnerability information shared broadly across critical infrastructure sectors until the patch was made available. Rather than engage in public-private partnership, these Federal agencies unilaterally decided to leave U.S. critical infrastructure owners and operators with limited visibility and awareness to ongoing, active attacks exploiting a 0-day vulnerability. However, indicators that could have helped cyber defenders (for example hashes of files related to the attack) could have aided critical infrastructure to identify if they were under attack and take response actions. This could be done without leaking sensitive information that could lead to additional threat actors exploiting the vulnerability. Critical infrastructure protection and resiliency did not appear to be the priority for these agencies.

Finally, almost 3 weeks later, vulnerability and patch information was released as TLP:WHITE information along with a TLP:AMBER Joint Cybersecurity Advisory with information related to the attack. Then over a week later, similar information was released as TLP:WHITE. Then after another week went by, without coordinating or notifying the victim organization ahead of time, CISA personnel named the victim in a public Senate hearing and a USCG TLP:AMBER Technical Report was leaked to the press. During this time no Federal agency contacted or collaborated with the MTS–ISAC or other National Council of ISAC members. However, the MTS–ISAC regularly shares Cybersecurity Advisories with personnel at all 3 agencies and is a member of CISA's Cyber Information Sharing and Collaboration Program (CISCP).

Trust is critical when fostering collaboration and information sharing, which we absolutely need to create a more cyber resilient critical infrastructure community. The maritime community's trust in Federal agencies was shaken following this incident because:

1. Immediately following the incident, the Federal Government delayed information sharing for 3 weeks while the critical infrastructure community was ready to share this information immediately.
2. CISA released the name of the victim which may have been in violation of the Cybersecurity Information Sharing Act of 2015 (CISA 2015) and perhaps the Federal Government should research whether this should lead to sanctions. "Section 1504(a)(3)(C)(ii) requires that procedures ensure there are appropriate sanctions in place for officers, employees, or agents of a Federal entity who

knowingly and willfully conduct activities under CISA 2015 in an unauthorized manner."[5]

3. A USCG For Official Use Only Technical Report with details surrounding the incident was leaked to the press. The MTS–ISAC did not receive this report nor did other maritime stakeholders. If the report was intended solely for the victim, then how did the press receive it? Some industry stakeholders are wondering if this was "leaked" as part of a political agenda. No matter how or why, several stakeholders have expressed concerns with reporting incidents to the government as a result.

To be honest, the most common refrain I hear from private-sector stakeholders when it comes to information sharing with the Federal Government can be boiled down to a lack of trust in how the Government will handle the information. I hate to hear this having served on active duty and as a Federal Government civilian, but there are some legitimate concerns that should be recognized. I thought about whether to bring this challenge up in my testimony, but nothing will improve by not bringing this up. At some point conversations about how Federal Government actions are undermining the trust of the critical infrastructure community would be healthy, in my opinion.

IV. Opportunities for Improvement

There are opportunities for the Federal Government to effectively partner with the MTS–ISAC and public and private-sector maritime stakeholders:

Improve Efficiencies

- Leverage ISACs and other forums to reduce redundant efforts and join private-sector stakeholders in their chosen collaboration mechanisms. The MTS–ISAC has non-voting seats for CISA, Coast Guard, and the Department of Energy representatives which remain unfilled by these agencies.

---

[5] https://www.cisa.gov/sites/default/files/publications/Cybersecurity%20Information%20-Sharing%20Act%20of%202015.pdf.

- Support private-sector stakeholder solutions that already address Federal Governmental needs and have proven effective for critical infrastructure.
- A great example is also the Information Exchanges being created that include port authorities, USCG, CISA, other agencies and public and private local Maritime stakeholders working with the MTS–ISAC at a community level to define and foster trust while sharing actionable, relevant, and timely threat information.

Information and Intelligence Sharing

- CISA 2015 remains significantly underutilized. Although it has been implemented, there remains resistance to fully trusting and using the provisions of the legislation by both Federal and private partnership programs.
- Prioritize ongoing bidirectional exchange of unclassified threat information between the public and private sectors, not just incident reporting.
- Holistic sharing of threat information, best practices, and lessons learned is more beneficial for improving cyber resilience than focused incident reporting.
- Improve training of Government personnel on proper information classification procedures and how to more effectively mark information to allow for sharing.
- Focus additional Federal resources toward information declassification efforts.

Resource Investments

- Ensure requirements are in place to raise awareness of Federal employees of cybersecurity funding opportunities that align with agency mission sets.[6]

---

[6] As an example, cybersecurity was the highest stated priority for FEMA's 2020 Port Security Grant Program. Yet many stakeholder requests for cybersecurity investments were turned down by USCG Captains of the Port in favor of physical security efforts, resulting in only roughly $12 million out of the $100 million program being invested in the highest priority area.

- Review opportunities for partnering with ISACs for hands-on cybersecurity training, internships, and educational opportunities.
- CISA should consider funding ISAC analyst positions at CISA Central to better facilitate the bi-directional flow of information across critical infrastructure.
- Multiple maritime stakeholders are partnering with Computer Science, Cybersecurity or other closely-related college programs to provide students with realworld experiences that they might not otherwise have exposure to for several years. These programs would benefit from further support and resourcing.
- Increase funding for voluntary programs such as RVAs, VADR, and CPTs; wait lists and backlogs for these efforts should not be reaching 18+ months as they have in the past. The Coast Guard has an outstanding Cyber Protection Team, but there is a need for regional cyber incident response teams. There are not enough to adequately provide assistance should there be even a mild demand. CISA was not able to respond in a timely manner to produce meaningful input to a recent attack on a port authority.

V. Conclusion

The MTS–ISAC is hopeful that the maritime critical infrastructure community and the Federal Government can more effectively partner with each other to safeguard our National interests. Sharing cyber threat information is a key element to improving our resiliency, and that will work best if industry and ISACs are engaged as envisioned by CISA 2015. Whether it is related to incident response or proactive threat information sharing, we need true collaboration between the Federal Government and other public and private-sector organizations. Currently this is not an effective system of public-private partnership and collaboration. It feels like industry is being threatened with additional regulation and security directives rather than being treated as the partners who own and operate the vast majority of critical infrastructure. I kindly request you consider the beneficial role that ISACs play daily in facilitating trusted, anonymous, information sharing for the improved resiliency of critical infrastructure across our country in the face of ongoing cyberattacks. Please include, and protect the mechanisms safeguarding, the ISAC communities in legislation related to critical infrastructure cybersecurity efforts. Any bill associated with critical infrastructure cybersecurity efforts that does not reflect the positive, critical, and irreplaceable role that ISACs and industry representatives and stakeholders provide to our critical infrastructure communities, and does not include provisions requiring Federal agencies to effectively collaborate with them, should be opposed. Thank you again for the opportunity to provide this testimony.

Ms. CLARKE. I thank you, Mr. Dickerson, for your testimony here today.

I thank all of our witnesses for their testimony.

Pursuant to today's order, the Chair declares the committees in recess, subject to the call of the Chair. Members will be given notification prior to reconvening after votes.

[Recess.] [3:59 p.m.].

Ms. CLARKE. Let me, first of all, thank all of our witnesses for your indulgence today. Just so happened that we had one of those rare or common conflicts of having votes in the middle of our hearing. So I truly appreciate your willingness to remain tuned in, and we will move forward now with questioning.

I will remind the subcommittees that we will each have 5 minutes to question the panel.

I will now recognize myself for questions. My first question is directed to Ms. Spaulding.

Ms. Spaulding, for many years, the Federal Government has relied on voluntary partnerships and programs to improve cybersecurity for critical infrastructure. Recent cyberattacks like Colonial Pipeline have forced a new conversation about whether that voluntary partnership model is sufficient for today's threat landscape. As the former under secretary for CISA's predecessor organization, could you talk about the limitations of the voluntary framework and the challenge of regulation in an area as dynamic as cybersecurity?

Ms. SPAULDING. Absolutely, Madam Chairwoman. Thank you. Both your points are very well taken. We are in a situation now where we have both the capability—I think we have reached a level of maturity in Government and in industry in understanding some of the basic things that really must be done and can be done to significantly raise the level of cybersecurity. So we are in a better position than we have been in the past in knowing what kinds of mandates to put in place. So that is one thing.

Then we do have a threat environment that continues to grow more and more grave with each passing day, and there is lots of evidence of this. We don't have access to the intelligence that the Government or TSA may have, although I think that TSA has briefed some of the companies about the intelligence that they are seeing that gives them that sense of urgency.

But even with what we see in open source in the media every day, it is very clear that our adversaries are very focused on our industrial control systems, on operational technology, and understanding that so that they can be in a position to disrupt it, and that criminal gangs are getting increasingly brazen in their targets with respect to ransomware, for example. But you can see it is grave.

Ms. CLARKE. So in your testimony—yes. So in your testimony, you mention that you are thinking it changed about the need to move from a voluntary to regulatory framework. What role do you see CISA playing as the long-time voluntary partner and civilian hub for cyber expertise in this shift?

Ms. SPAULDING. Yes. So CISA is thought to be, for example, the repository of mandatory reporting information that comes in. We need to have a place in Government that takes that information and adds value to it and makes sure that it is anonymous, but that it is analyzed, put in context, and then shared broadly, very quickly, so that everyone can use that information to better defend their networks.

CISA brings a couple decades now of expertise on cybersecurity and on these infrastructure sectors, and work in close collaboration with sector-specific agencies like TSA can really leverage that cybersecurity expertise to help the sector experts to find the right path forward in close collaboration and partnership with industry.

Ms. CLARKE. So this is to all of our witnesses, and I only have a minute and some change left, so if I don't get to you, if you would just submit something to us in writing, that will be helpful as well. But many of you mentioned the importance of mandatory cyber incident reporting as a way to grow visibility around cyber threats and improve the quality of bidirectional information sharing with the private sector. As you know, this is a top priority of mine.

Ms. Spaulding, if a mandatory cyber incident reporting regime had been in place at CISA since you were under secretary, what security gains might have been made since that time?

Ms. SPAULDING. So two things I would point to. That information can be shared more broadly so that all network defenders have a better sense of the tactics, techniques, and procedures they are defending against. No. 2, it would help to calculate a return on security investment so that CISOs at companies all across the country can make the case more effectively for that investment. So I do believe it would have raised our cybersecurity posture.

Ms. CLARKE. Ms. Cogswell, can you elaborate on how cyber incident reporting could be used to improve security for industrial control systems across sectors?

Ms. COGSWELL. One of the most important things I have seen is that ability to bring information, like mandatory cyber reporting information, with your industry experts and to be able to use and engage with that information in a way that helps you propose a next level of solutions. The additional reporting, the ability to see how it operates in one area, how therefore it might appear in another area in advance of that area being a target can be really quite powerful. I have seen a lot of really great work when you have Government and industry sitting together engaging with that type of data.

Ms. CLARKE. Thank you very much.

I now recognize the Ranking Member, Mr. Garbarino, of the Subcommittee on Cybersecurity, Infrastructure, and Innovation, the gentleman from New York, for questions at this time.

Mr. GARBARINO. Thank you, Chairwoman. Thank you to the people testifying today, the witnesses.

My first question is for Mr. Dickerson. Can you please discuss the unique complications of the maritime environment and how ports must often comply with multiple regulations and requirements from the Coast Guard, TSA, and others? Can you describe some of the specific challenges when it comes to securing ports?

Mr. DICKERSON. Thank you, Congressman Garbarino, for that question. It is highly complex environment where, because of the intermodal aspects of the maritime sector, you will have port authorities, for example, owning the last mile of rail. So then they need to comply with TSA's upcoming rail security directive.

Similarly, they will also own pipelines. So now it becomes a question of, OK, are we reporting this information to TSA, to the U.S. Coast Guard, CISA? Do we need to involve FBI? Some of these might require CBP reporting due to goods coming into the ports. It becomes a mesh of Federal agencies that then need that required reporting.

Again, as I mentioned earlier in my testimony, that can lead to a lot of redundant efforts and really pulling the cyber defenders away from incident response to now answering multiple questions from multiple agencies at a time when they really need to be focused on those response actions.

Mr. GARBARINO. OK. So maybe for you and the—all the panelists. So what recommendations in detail do you have to better harmonize these requirements?

Mr. DICKERSON. I think one of the things——

Mr. GARBARINO. I mean, one—so it is not so—not just so that it works with industry, so it is not a high burden on industry, but also—but still sets a high cybersecurity standard.

Mr. DICKERSON. Right. So I think part of the question is, is there a centralized point, belly button, for that reporting? If that is formally the NCIC on the SIOC, CISA central, and you have representatives from those agencies there, or if you have CISA representatives at those agencies, I think there is options for either way to then correlate some of that information, make sure it gets to all of the right agencies and partners, but that then you are not having to report the same information, answer the same questions over and over, if that helps, sir.

Mr. GARBARINO. Nope, that does.

Anything else from any other panelists, or I can go to my next question? Anybody want to add anything?

All right. If nothing, this is pretty much for everybody, so jump in when you want. As the Federal Government sets the standards for industrial control systems' cybersecurity in collaboration with the critical infrastructure community, there will inevitably be requirements for companies to validate the controls in place, as we saw in the TSA security directive.

What is the most effective way to, in a scalable manner, have these validations take place? Should TSA conduct them, CISA? Or can DHS, TSA, and the industry agree on what comprises a cybersecurity validation and have private companies do it?

That is—and whoever wants to jump in first if you have——

Ms. COGSWELL. I will be happy to start. I will say that I think this is an environment where there are a number of opportunities to engage across the board. As you noted, there are existing protocols by which TSA and CISA partner for the validated architecture reviews, but at the same time, there are models under which regulatorily you can create the opportunity for third-party entities who are off an improved list, clearly qualified and found to be—to meet various standards who can also perform those types of services.

As I noted in my opening statement, one such model that TSA has actually used before is the third-party canine program, where they create an approved list of canine operators who can be used in screening operations. They therefore can regulate both the entity that is providing the service as well as the entity who is using it, to make sure that the goals and outcomes are reaching everybody's desired end-state.

This is an area I think that should be explored. I think there is huge opportunity, frankly, to expand the number of entities who can participate, which helps all of us, so that you are not worried so much about necessarily limited resources at any one point, or, frankly, you know, every company not having to come up to speed on every nuance of cyber, which may be more difficult given the difficulties in hiring cyber talent these days in particular.

Mr. GARBARINO. Yes. Difficulties and expense.

OK. I appreciate it. So we would be better off doing a third party. I appreciate your answer.

If nobody else has anything else back, I do yield—has anything else to say, I do yield back to the Chairwoman.

Ms. CLARKE. I thank you, Ranking Member Garbarino.

I now recognize the Chairwoman of the Subcommittee on Transportation and Maritime Security, the gentlelady from New Jersey, Mrs. Watson Coleman, for her questions at this time.

Mrs. WATSON COLEMAN. Thank you, Chairwoman. Thank you to all of our witnesses.

In 2001, terrorists needed to make it onto the planes and into the cockpit in order to execute the 9/11 attack. However, in 2021, we must also consider the possibility that a terrorist or hostile nation could hijack a flight by hacking it, without ever passing through TSA checkpoints or stepping foot on that plane.

Mr. Troy, Ms. Spaulding, and Ms. Cogswell, would you comment on this: As aircraft become increasingly connected and automated, how do we prevent hackers from hijacking planes and, in worstcase scenario, if a hijacker obtained operational control, what redundancies should we have in place to ensure that a real pilot can regain control? What role do you see TSA and CISA, in concert with FAA, ensuring the security of aircraft operational control and navigational systems?

I will start with you, Mr. Troy, Ms. Spaulding, and then Ms. Cogswell, please.

Mr. TROY. Thank you. Excellent question. So the aviation industry has an incredible safety record based on strong engineering design and continuous enhancement, and the aviation industry does recognize cybersecurity as a critical part of aviation safety. So the industry has an incredible safety record, and it is the result of careful incorporation of functionality and strong secure system design. The airplane design is based on careful system integration and system isolation as appropriate and redundancy for critical systems. So safety critical systems are highly protected and hardened against attacks, but we are continuously evaluating the changing cyber threat space and trying to incorporate then improvements to anticipate threats. So the systems are separated from cyber and system engineering reasons as well.

With respect to your question about a hacker obtaining operational control. As I stated above, the planes are designed with redundant systems such that if a system is not operating as designed, another system can be engaged to perform the function. Pilots are trained as well to address system failures and, ultimately, pilots are a critical layer of protection for continued safe flight and landing.

With respect to the question on TSA and CISA and their roles, as well as FAA, they are all stakeholders in the safety of aircraft, as are airlines, and, you know, being operators of the aircraft. These Government agencies should be working with the manufacturers to obtain assurance that the aircraft, as designed, are periodically assessed against threats. These Government agencies are also incredibly helpful in sharing threat intelligence information.

Mrs. WATSON COLEMAN. Thank you. Ms. Spaulding.

Ms. SPAULDING. Yes. I can vouch for my days at DHS that the industry takes this threat very seriously and that there is close interagency cooperation. Of course, DHS and FAA and DOD are all members of the Aviation Cybersecurity Initiative working closely with industry.

I do think it is something that requires constant reassessment, constant monitoring, to make sure that the design basis that Jeff talks about is up-to-date, is keeping up with everything that we know about the nature of the threat, and that that industry-Government collaboration continue to be very strong. This is a very dynamic field.

Mrs. WATSON COLEMAN. Thank you. Ms. Cogswell.

Ms. COGSWELL. Thank you very much. As you know, the Transportation Security Administration actually started as part of the Department of Transportation. As such, we have very close, strong ties with the FAA and other sister entities within the Department of Transportation that continue to this day. On any given day, talk 12, 15 times, conduct regular exercises, share information on threats.

I will say one of the things that I want to highlight that Suzanne noted is that continuing focus on looking at what is next on the horizon and how do we best make sure that we use our compatible authorities, safety and security, to take the best action with these threats.

I will say, during my time at TSA, we also worked very closely together and then with industry on those problems where we saw a nexus crossing over between the agencies.

Similarly, CISA, given their membership in DHS as a strong partner from that front, proved valuable in a number of these conversations to help articulate and describe different angles against which we should be looking at that threat. I feel confident these conversations continue.

Mrs. WATSON COLEMAN. Thank you. Madam Chairwoman, I yield back.

Ms. CLARKE. The Chair now recognizes the Ranking Member of the Subcommittee on Transportation, Maritime—and Maritime Subcommittee, the gentleman from Florida, Mr. Gimenez.

Let me just state that, going forward, Mrs. Watson Coleman will be presiding on the balance of our hearing this afternoon. Thank you very much.

I yield to the gentleman from Florida.

I assume that the gentleman from Florida has not returned as of yet, so I am going to turn the meeting over—the hearing over to my colleague, if she is ready at this time.

Mrs. WATSON COLEMAN [presiding.] Thank you, Madam Chairwoman.

I am trying to see who is next. I believe it is Representative Jackson Lee from Texas. I am sorry, I am getting this information in live time.

Ms. CLARKE. OK.

Mrs. WATSON COLEMAN. Representative Jackson Lee.

Ms. CLARKE. She is—I think she is trying to unmute.

Ms. JACKSON LEE. Thank you. The staff has to do so. Thank you, Madam Chair. We can't self—under the Webex Cisco, we cannot self-unmute ourselves.

But let me thank both of you and the Ranking Member for these important messages that we have been gathering today, and I am going to ask a question of all.

I think it was, Mr. Troy, your testimony, I think, suggested there was a lot of layering with respect to Governmental regulation and addition, and your point would be that we need to find a way to be more specific and pointed.

Am I correct, Mr. Troy? Was that your testimony, or Mr. Dickerson?

Mr. DICKERSON. Congresswoman Jackson Lee, I had some comments on those lines. This is Mr. Dickerson.

Ms. JACKSON LEE. OK. So would you expand on how we can be more effective regulators first? Then I have one or two other questions. But can you quickly respond to how we can be more effective in our work? This is important work and important infrastructure that needs to be secured. So, Mr. Troy?

Mr. TROY. So I believe that one of the things that is really important as we look at putting out mandatory reporting and regulations on the industry is that we use a phased approach. A phased approach basically is one that ensures that all of the people who are going to fall under these requirements can achieve the success of getting these requirements in place.

When we look at what they have done, for example, on the Department of Defense with the defense contractors, there has been, you know, a ramp-up of increased cybersecurity maturity requirements of all the defense contractors. I think a lot of great lessons have been learned from that process, and by establishing baseline controls and then continuing to evaluate the ability of industry to meet those and then challenge them and bring them up higher is an effective process.

Ms. JACKSON LEE. Let me ask—thank you so very much. Let me ask further witnesses.

Ms. Spaulding, I want to focus on trains—trains in the Eastern Corridor, trains that go really into neighborhoods. I really think that we have been on the edge of good luck, in all honesty, in terms of dealing with trains that—purposefully so, they were meant to go almost up to your front door. They go behind homes. These are interstate trains. Homes are built right on the back side of trains. They are in mountains, they are in valleys, they are in dangerous places, and they are Amtrak.

What are special efforts that specifically look at trains and the cyber system dealing with ultimately—if I could use the terminology—the massive train wreck that could come from a cyber failure on our train systems? There is interstate train system and then obviously the computer—excuse me—the commuter train. Would you care to comment on that?

Ms. SPAULDING. Absolutely, Congresswoman. Your points about the potential risks that come with our rail system across the country is exactly right. The good news is that the rail industry has worked closely with DHS for many years. When I was the under secretary at DHS, the Rail Sector Coordinating Council was very active, and they have done a lot, both in the physical safety arena and security arena, and cybersecurity.

But as you point out, it is a complex system, and we now know what are the basic things that really need to be done across the board to protect and defend and make more resilient these critical assets and systems. Sometimes you have got to issue a mandate in order to make sure that everyone, not just those who are actively involved, but that everyone that is controlling, owning, and operating sensitive assets comes up to at least that basic standard of care, and then, very importantly, has plans in place to deal with any incident that might arise to reduce the impact and the harm to the American public and to our economy.

Ms. JACKSON LEE. Thank you.

Let me just quickly, on the—combine pipeline and planes together and just say, one of the things that we have looked at over the years is the apron, the back side of the airport, which, at that time, there was intrusion by uninvited guests, potential terrorists, because it was so vulnerable in the back.

But there are also the apron of a cybersecurity system as relates to flights, maybe even as it relates to the air traffic arena, but also the airlines that sort of run their own systems, and they have a cyber system now far different than this——

Mrs. WATSON COLEMAN. The gentlelady's time has expired. I will let you finish your comment, though. Thank you.

Ms. JACKSON LEE. Thank you. Thank you so very much.

So, in the future, if you could answer the question about that back side of the airport, and then as well, to tie the pipeline question into my rail question, which is pipelines are everywhere as well and do we have the adequate cyber protection for pipelines that wind up in our backyards?

I would yield back. If Madam Chair—I don't know if someone can answer it in very short period. I don't know. I would welcome that. Thank you. If anyone can answer those.

Mr. TROY. Yes. Very quickly, when you mention a back side of the airport, it makes me think so, really, the operational technologies that help an airport run.

Ms. JACKSON LEE. Right.

Mr. TROY. That is a very big focus of the airlines and the airports right now as they look at both the common suppliers to those particular types of technologies and the potential vulnerabilities as well.

Mrs. WATSON COLEMAN. Thank you, Mr. Troy. Thank you, Ms. Jackson Lee.

Ms. JACKSON LEE. Thank you very much.

Mrs. WATSON COLEMAN. I now recognize Mr. Clyde of Georgia.

Mr. CLYDE. Thank you, Madam Chairwoman. I appreciate that. My question is for Mr. Troy. As you well know, if the aviation sector were to experience a cyberattack, it could very well have a devastating impact on the security of our Nation and our economy.

So, in your opinion, what is the greatest area of cyber threat in aviation? If I could have your opinion on that.

Is it the airport itself? Is it the—I mean, you talked a little bit about the planes. I think Madam Chairwoman discussed that. Then you also have the airlines themselves with, indeed, their own systems. You know, any part of that could shut down air travel across the United States in various different sectors.

What is your opinion, what is our greatest cyber threat when it comes to the aviation side?

Mr. TROY. That is a great question, and it is very difficult to answer because of the interconnectivity of the aviation system. It is really an ecosystem.

So if I am running an airline, I am very concerned that if I land my planes into my hub airport and that airport can't function, that creates a problem for me. If I am that airport, and I have the same problem if all those airlines are parked at my gates and they can't move because of some function that they are unable to perform.

So I am not trying to cop out on your question, but I really think it speaks exactly to why our industry needs to work so well together, because of this shared risk within supply chain and the industry segments that make up the aviation ecosystem.

Mr. CLYDE. OK. That is kind-of the area I am going to here because, looking at aviation, I just see that as a—you know, such a low-hanging fruit, because, as of yet, I have not really heard of a cyberattack on aviation that really had any effect. You know, it is a fantastic thing, and that is wonderful, but that means it just hasn't showed up yet.

So would any of our other witnesses want to chime in on what the aviation industry is doing or what the greatest vulnerability might be and how we could assist in mitigating that vulnerability?

Ms. COGSWELL. I am happy to sort-of build on the answer that was presented, which I completely agree with. I think one of the most undervalued points that has come from all of this is understanding how an impact to one part of a system can ripple across and affect the system as a whole. Taking that information and going back into the various individual company systems and those interconnected systems and better assessing what would that look like, and how do we make sure that we are quickly able to contain it and mitigate it should we see that start to occur.

Not the same at all, but I will draw a comparison to when Gatwick was actually shut down for several days because of unmanned aerial systems flying overhead. As you recall, they didn't actually harm anything, but they had periodic events where they just kept coming into the area. That clearly made it unsafe to fly, right? So they grounded all of the planes in the airport. It shut down that airport. It shut down flow to connecting airport.

Exactly as my colleague just said, big ripple effects, even for something that was not actually a kinetic, physical accident or disruption that they might think of seeing otherwise. Truly important for us as a model to understand that kind of interconnected model and how we can collectively work to defend our systems.

Mr. CLYDE. Well, thank you. Thank you very much. I appreciate your comments, Ms. Cogswell.

That is my great concern, and I appreciate each of you bringing your ideas to light.

With that, Madam Chairwoman, I yield back.

Mrs. WATSON COLEMAN. Thank you very much.

The gentlelady from New York, Miss Rice, is recognized for 5 minutes.

Miss RICE. Thank you so much, Madam Chair. I am so grateful for this hearing.

You know, listening to this conversation brings me back to 9/11. As a New Yorker, we felt the pain of that attack very intimately. I remember, in the days and weeks and months after 9/11, you know, which basically shut down the aviation industry for some time, and I remember wondering whether we are ever going to come back. Are people ever going to feel comfortable flying again? Of course they did. But during that interim period, there was thoughts in, you know, law enforcement that what is going to be next? Like, what—the terrorists showed how they could attack us here on American soil and do it in a way that shut down an entire industry that had an enormous economic impact on our country for a long time.

And I remember, you know, talking to my friends in law enforcement in New York at that time, and they were thinking, gosh, do we have to worry about someone just walking into a mall, 3 or 4 different malls across this country? You want to talk about shutting down day-to-day economic activity. Make people afraid to even leave their homes.

I think what we are—the subject matter of today's hearing brings me to that—again to that issue of how we get people around safely and efficiently and all those things that our economy can hum, but we also do it in a way that keeps people safe.

So, Ms. Spaulding, I mean, I think it is pretty obvious why a mass transit system would be of interest to a foreign adversary. Up to this point, we haven't seen one that has had a massive safety impact, you know, but I guess my question is: How do we—you know, I worry about these transportation systems, because some of them are run by Governmental agencies and others are privately-run.

So when you are looking to come up with a system of protocols to keep us safe and prevent, whether it is cyberattacks or any other kind of attack, on our transportation system, how do we set up a system that can apply equally and effectively—as effectively to both the public and private sector?

Ms. SPAULDING. Yes, it is a great question. Your point about, you know, the aviation industry in the wake of 9/11, you know, is a reminder that—of the way in which an incident one place, in one part of an industry can destroy public trust in the entire industry. Again, one of the reasons that, you know, it is in these sectors' best interests to ensure that all of the players owning and operating key assets are brought up to a baseline level of cybersecurity to protect the public trust in that entire industry.

In terms of government, you know, are you—our critical infrastructure is, we always say, owned 85 percent by the private sector. Nobody knows what the exact percentage is, but that means that other percent is publicly-owned. There are a number of ways in which industry and Government come together. There are—for government-owned utilities as well as private sector.

There is a multi-State ISAC that is for the States to come together to share best practices, including around operational technology they own. There is a government coordinating council that includes State and local and territorial and Tribal government for governments to come together to talk about the things that they own. All of the various sectors that have coordinating committees have a government counterpart.

So the mechanisms are there. You are absolutely right; as with every other area, we need to make sure we are harmonizing the requirements and that we are looking across these industries regardless of who owns them, because our adversaries are doing exactly that.

Miss RICE. Absolutely. You know, I know this is going to sound like a political pitch. It really is not meant to be, but, you know, our transportation security, there is a cyber—certainly a very profound cybersecurity aspect to it, but there is also an infrastructure aspect to it as well.

Do we have the—are our transportation systems as up-to-date and resilient and safe as they need to be? I know my Republican colleagues on this call feel the same way that I do, that, you know, major investment in our infrastructure shows not just Americans that they should be able to travel safely and feel confident in the way that they travel around this country and around the world, but it sends a very clear message to our adversaries that we are investing in our infrastructure and so they should beware. So thank you all so much for coming today. It is a great conversation. I yield back the balance of my time.

Mrs. WATSON COLEMAN. I thank the gentlelady.

I now recognize the gentleman and Ranking Member from Florida, Mr. Gimenez, for 5 minutes.

Mr. GIMENEZ. Thank you, Madam Chair.

I am going to kind-of focus in on an area that has got me concerned.

Mr. Dickerson, do you have, off the top of your head, either the correct number or maybe a guesstimate of the percentage of cranes that are utilized by U.S. ports that are made in China?

Mr. DICKERSON. Thank you, Congressman Gimenez. I do not have that, but it is a pretty significant number for those ship-to- shore gantry cranes that we rely on to move the goods from ships to shore and vice versa.

Mr. GIMENEZ. I have two concerns about that. No. 1, I know that in the Port of Miami, we do have some Chinese cranes, and we know that we had concerns about embedded in the software that came with the cranes was malware that was meant to penetrate the port systems and do whatever it was that the Chinese wanted to do with our port operating systems. That is one concern.

The other concern that I have is that, whenever the Chinese want, they can cut off our supply of spare parts, which means that a significant portion of our ability to load and offload ships will be compromised if that were the case.

Do you know—do you have any thoughts on how we can mitigate the risk of infiltration into our port systems via these cranes and other either new or existing, you know, technologies at ports and infrastructure that ports need?

Mr. DICKERSON. Thank you again, sir. I think there is a few things, and those are very valid concerns. One is the ability to be able to conduct risk assessments immediately on that equipment. So CISA has the vulnerability architecture designer's views, data, program. But, quite honestly, often that is perhaps a 12- to 18- month waiting list period before you can actually conduct that review. In those cases, we need that equipment operational immediately upon arrival. There is not necessarily that time to waste. So then it is an opportunity to perhaps engage in, as was mentioned earlier, some prequalified private-sector vendors that might be able to help augment CISA's functionality to conduct those reviews so that they can be done in a timely manner, and we can then identify if there is any vulnerabilities that need to be addressed.

Mr. GIMENEZ. Well, do you think that maybe we need to wean ourselves off of this dependence on Chinese technology that, again, comes from a sole source that could be our adversary?

I actually believe that it is the biggest threat that we have, is the ascendancy of China, that they could basically cut off our supply of spare parts and grind this country to a halt in terms of its import and export capabilities. So, in light of that, I am going to be introducing some legislation about that. We need other sources that are either allies or friendly nations and not so much of it coming from one source with China.

I understand what China did. They undercut everybody else in the world, and basically they are the sole provider of cranes around the world, which makes them a—I think it is a very, very dangerous practice and a very, very dangerous situation we have in the United States. Would you agree with that?

Mr. DICKERSON. Yes, sir. I think there is some undercutting of the market taking place, and so having alternative sources and then being able to augment that with perhaps some grant programs that could allow then the private sector to make those investments reasonably would be helpful.

Mr. GIMENEZ. OK. Like I said, I will be introducing some legislation to try and wean us off of these Chinese cranes and other infrastructure needs at our ports that may be coming from adversary nations.

With that, my time is up, and thank you, Madam Chairwoman. I yield back.

Mrs. WATSON COLEMAN. Thank you.

I now recognize the gentlelady from Las Vegas, Ms. Titus.

Ms. TITUS. Thank you, Madam Chairman. A very interesting——

Mrs. WATSON COLEMAN. From Nevada. I am sorry. Nevada.

Ms. TITUS. Nevada.

Mrs. WATSON COLEMAN. I shouldn't be so myopic.

Ms. TITUS. That is all right. We answer to just about anything. I wanted to address this question to Ms. Spaulding. You know, McCarran Airport in my district, Las Vegas, sees just thousands of passengers every year. We are probably the only airport that has got slot machines, so a lot of them are playing slot machines. But a lot of them are working on their computers while they are waiting for their flights.

I just wonder if you would address the need for security on those airport WiFis, because a lot of personal data is being floated around that we don't know if that is safe or not. Furthermore, when they get on the plane, they use the plane's WiFi. One of the biggest complaints is when the flight attendant says, "Our WiFi is down," you can hear all the groans and the Candy Crush players and all of that.

But could you address the issue of securing that kind of WiFi, either in the airport or on the planes where people are connecting to it and exposing a lot of personal data?

Ms. SPAULDING. Yes. Congresswoman, you are exactly right. We have all known that those public WiFi—free public WiFi availability in places like airports is completely insecure, and certainly have advised the public as best we can to be aware of that and not to use those.

But, realistically, they are going to continue to take advantage of the connectivity that is available to them. I think it is a very good point that those systems ought to be more secured. It is very difficult to have something that is open to a very transient population, right, coming and going, where you cannot use the security protocols that you can with a work force that is more stationary. So I don't mean to minimize the challenge, but I think it is something that we should be moving toward.

In the meantime, I hope that the public is watching and hearing how, at the moment, how unsecure those networks are.

Ms. TITUS. Well, thank you. I hope so too. I wish people were just reading books instead of playing computer games, but that is just my practice.

Along those same lines, a number of the airports have vendors that take your very personal data, and we see a lot of that at McCarran, like with the prevetting of customers. They take eyes— you know, you look in and you see your eyes and biometric data, and so I would think they would need some pretty high standards of cybersecurity.

I don't know if they are doing that. If you can comment on that, you and Ms. Cogswell, and how TSA is dealing with that.

Ms. SPAULDING. So I know that Patricia will have some insights on this as well. I am familiar with some of those vendors that are providing some of that vetting before you board the plane, for example, to speed you through the lines. They know that—how absolutely vital it is that they keep that information secure. That is very personal information. So my sense is they take cybersecurity very seriously. But I will see if Patricia has more to add.

Ms. TITUS. Thank you.

Ms. COGSWELL. Thank you very much for the question. I have actually been spending quite a bit of time on this since my departure from Government, working with—across the industry—airlines, airports, technology vendors, associations, and others about how we can encourage, frankly, an environment that holistically supports innovation for aviation passenger experience, making it, frankly, from couch to gate, a more pleasant experience, one that offers many different opportunities.

You are exactly right that there is a strong recognition that we need to embed several key things along the way, one of which is that cybersecurity protection so that people feel confident and comfortable about what is happening with their data. Along with that is the press also to make sure that there is a better recognition and a better way to have these vendors tell people what are they collecting, who are they sending it to, are they storing it, and how is it being used?

So all of these, I think, will form a core that we are hoping to continue to look to progress in this environment. There are standards that are used today. CBP has published a standard that is used by CBP and TSA for a number of those pilots that you are talking about where the biometric is collected and transmitted to use either for access to a lounge or to board the plane or go through security.

There are also additional new emerging standards, such as the mobile driver's license recently announced by TSA and Apple that also are coming through in these areas.

Across the board, you are seeing an emphasis on that cybersecurity. I expect that to continue to evolve.

Your earlier point, given that all of these are operating in that WiFi-connected area, that also matters, that they need to look at it as a zero-trust environment where the network itself is not secure and, therefore, the information needs to be secure while it is in transmission.

Ms. TITUS. Well, thank you so much.

Thank you, Madam Chairman. Maybe we can look into this.

Mrs. WATSON COLEMAN. Thank you very much.

I now recognize the gentleman from New Jersey, Mr. Van Drew.

Mr. VAN DREW. Thank you, Madam Chair. It is good to see you. This is a question for Mr. Dickerson. Mr. Dickerson, as you may know, roughly 5.4 trillion flows through the Maritime Transportation System each and every year, which compromises about 25— comprises, rather, about 25 percent of the United States' gross domestic product.

The MTS consists of an intricate network of waterways, ships, ports, and terminals, and intermodal landline connections, which allow various modes of transportation to move goods and to move people. The Coast Guard is the lead Federal agency for regulation of the MTS, and it currently has the relationships, the regulatory authority, and the response capabilities to prevent and respond to threats throughout the system.

So my first question for you is: How can we best use the Coast Guard's existing relationships at the port level to improve our ability to manage cyber risk with the MTS?

Mr. DICKERSON. Thank you, Congressman Van Drew. There is a couple of things that can be done. We already have the Area Maritime Security Committees that are active in almost all the captain of the port areas with a cybersecurity subcommittee that addresses risks. Currently, those are supported by a variety of folks with different skill levels when it comes to cybersecurity and knowledge levels at the Coast Guard level. But they are trying to hire more MTS cyber specialists into each captain of the port area which could then support those Area Maritime Security Committees.

With those committees, you have both public and private-sector stakeholders that are engaged, and they can be involved in risk planning, exercises, et cetera. One of the things the MTS–ISAC is doing, we have formed a number of information exchanges with those local stakeholders to make sure the public and private sectors are really aware of the day-to-day cyber threat activity that is targeting them.

So that helps bridge that gap between the AMSC, which might be more at a strategic level than the actual operational and tactical levels of cybersecurity that go on day-to-day. But that is definitely an area of focus that can be improved.

Thank you so much.

Mr. VAN DREW. Good. I think the Coast Guard can be very essential in this entire process, and as we move on and times change and things change, so does their role, and I think this is an area we really should focus on as well. I appreciate your answer.

I have another question for you. Members of the committee have received feedback that public-private partnerships are, unfortunately, sometimes turning into situations in which companies do give their information, as they should, to the Government, but they are not receiving anything meaningful in return. In other words, that collaboration that we want to see back and forth, I have heard, does not always exist. It should, because this is a very larger-than-life foe that we have to deal with here, and we all need to work together.

I was wondering what your thoughts on that were and how we can do better with that.

Mr. DICKERSON. Thank you, Congressman, again. Public-private partnerships are absolutely critical. This is—cyber is a team sport, and we all need to work together, absolutely. We need to work together cross-sector-wise as well, which is why the MTS–ISAC is part of the National Council of ISACs.

But when it comes to partnering with the Coast Guard, yes, we have received that feedback many times. Coast Guard receives the information, but then it might be months before any information is released from the Coast Guard back to the industry community. I think closer partnerships—and I am in multiple conversations with a number of Coast Guard leaders, and we are working on improving that public-private partnership, making sure that we can mature those procedures that are in place, to analyze the information, enrich it, and get it back from the Government in a more timely manner.

Mr. VAN DREW. I think they want to do that. I think there is really unexplored areas there that we can really do great things together. Coast Guard is a great agency, as you know, and I think they really can offer a great deal if we are working in tandem, if we are working in partnership. I thank you for your answers.

I yield back, Madam Chair.

Mr. DICKERSON. I completely agree. Thank you, sir.

Mrs. WATSON COLEMAN. Thank you, Mr. Van Drew. Thank you.

I now recognize the gentleman from New York, Mr. Torres, for 5 minutes.

Mr. TORRES. Thank you, Madam Chair.

You know, I have concerns that the United States for far too long has been complacent about cybersecurity instead of proactively securing critical infrastructure from cyber threats. The Federal Government is largely reacting to events. Colonial Pipeline is exhibit A. Before the breach of Colonial Pipeline, there were virtually no rules mandating pipeline cybersecurity. Only after the Colonial breach did the TSA finally issue security directives.

So as far as I am concerned, the breach of Colonial Pipeline demonstrates the laissez-faire approach to cybersecurity that the Federal Government has taken has been an abject failure.

My first question is for Ms. Spaulding about TSA. Instead of only issuing a security directive for each mode of transportation, should the TSA promulgate universal cybersecurity standards for all modes of critical transportation?

Ms. SPAULDING. It is a good question, Congressman. First of all, I think the security directives are a first step from TSA, and DHS has indicated that it is very likely to move to regulations. The security directives have a limited life span, and within a year or so, they have to be replaced. DHS has indicated it is likely to move to regulations.

That will allow for a formal notice and comment period. I think it is really important that there be some harmonization across sectors, as a number of the witnesses have noted. That is really important, particularly for companies that have assets that cross sectors. But I think there should be room—there may be need for some specialized requirements depending on the nature of the operations.

Mr. TORRES. I don't mean to—if I can interject for a moment. Obviously, there is a need for sector-specific standards, but there are best practices in cybersecurity that all individuals and institutions should adopt in both the public and private sector, whether it is the appointment of a CISO or multifactorial authentication or software updates or password updates or contingency planning.

So if we all—if those are universally agreed-upon best practices in cybersecurity, why not mandate them for all operators and owners of critical transportation infrastructure?

Ms. SPAULDING. Yes. You are absolutely right, Congressman. There is some basic cyber hygiene, we call it, that should be universal. I think the admonition that one of the witnesses made earlier, to do this in a phased approach makes sense. I think identifying what DHS has indicated is they are going to start with the most critical assets. I think that makes a lot of sense, to get the Government and industry to learn lessons about how to do this in terms of mandatory compliance with directives, how to monitor that, how to enforce that mandatory reporting. But, yes, you are absolutely right, there is a baseline of cybersecurity that ought to be universal.

Mr. TORRES. You mentioned reporting. The policy of cyber incident reporting raises the question, what exactly qualifies as a significant cyber incident, and there is a lack of clarity about the definition.

So take as an example the Colonial Pipeline. As you know, the breach of the pipeline led to the shutdown for a 5,500-mile pipeline that made up nearly half of the fuel supplies of the East Coast. It had economic effects that were felt on the ground: The closing of gas stations, panic buying, long lines.

Despite those effects, the Federal Government did not designate the Colonial breach as a significant cyber incident. Like, in what universe does that make sense? It seems strange to me.

Ms. SPAULDING. So the designation of a significant cyber incident is more of a signal to the Government about the need for an interagency, White House-led meeting to deal with the response, right? I think there is a legitimate question about what—where you should set the threshold, for example, for mandatory reporting, but ransomware, it seems to me, is an easy threshold to set.

Mr. TORRES. So do you agree with the Federal Government's decision not to designate the Colonial breach as a significant cyber incident? Because,

I mean, that situation, I mean, did implicate a number of agencies. It even reached the attention of the President himself. So it would seem to have all the hallmarks of a significant cyber incident.

Ms. SPAULDING. You know, Congressman, I am inclined to agree with you, is that the level of interagency meeting that was probably happening at the White House, it strikes me as probably very much the same as a significant cyber incident. I do think that should be separated from the thresholds that are set for mandatory reporting.

Mr. TORRES. I just feel like we need a greater sense of urgency and more common sense when it comes to cybersecurity policy in the Federal Government. So I will leave it at that.

Thank you.

Mrs. WATSON COLEMAN. Thank you, Mr. Torres.

I would like to recognize Mr. Langevin from Rhode Island for 5 minutes.

Mr. LANGEVIN. Thank you, Madam Chair. I have been on and off the hearing, so in between the meeting, so I thank you and the other Members for hosting the hearing. I really want to thank our witnesses for their testimony.

If I could start with Ms. Spaulding. First of all, Ms. Spaulding, I greatly appreciate your contributions to cyber and our National security writ large, both in your role at DHS and, of course, as one of our fellow commissioners on the Cyberspace Solarium Commission.

But let me just start with this. On October 19, several of the Senators sent a letter to TSA Administrator Pekoske encouraging him to reconsider using emergency authority for new transportation cybersecurity regulations in—and I quote, "the absence of an immediate threat."

So I am not sure if my colleagues were watching the news in May, but the Colonial Pipeline incident obviously disrupted the delivery of approximately half of the East Coast's fuel supply. Ransomware or other cyber intrusion against an air traffic control station or a mass transit system could be equally debilitating.

So I wanted to ask, if I could, do you believe TSA's new cybersecurity requirements on the rail—rail transit and aviation industries was warranted given the imminent threats that we face?

Ms. SPAULDING. Congressman, first, thank you for your kind words. Most importantly, thank you for your leadership over many years in cybersecurity, and it has been an honor to serve with you on the Cyberspace Solarium Commission.

I do believe that there is an emergency here, a sense of urgency. We are fortunate that TSA has this authority to be able to move quickly and that it has exercised that authority.

I think it is probably fair to say that, on May 6, Colonial Pipeline was not thinking that this was an urgent threat. In fact, there are reports that they had been putting off their vulnerability architecture design review. They just weren't getting around to it. That is the kind-of, you know, September 10 mindset that we are trying to avoid here.

We have so much evidence of this emergency, between the attacks in 2017 on safety systems that were clearly designed to be ready to inflict physical harm on people by disabling safety systems and operations. The Florida water treatment—the attack on the Florida water treatment facility, putting toxic levels of chemicals— trying to put toxic levels of chemicals into water. I think the sense of urgency should be palpable and felt by everyone by now.

Mr. LANGEVIN. Thank you. I would agree.

Let me turn to another line of questioning on third-party auditing. So again to you, the TSA pipeline security directives require baseline cybersecurity procedures such as reporting incidents, implementing multifactorial authentication, and developing and testing cyber contingency response plans. So in my view, these requirements are a good start, but more, candidly, should be done. I also believe that TSA should implement auditing of the cybersecurity controls covered entities have put in place.

So an impartial third-party auditor, such as a certified private-sector company or even CISA, would have both the impartiality and the on-network testing personnel necessary to ensure covered entities properly implement cybersecurity controls.

So from your experience and your perspective, do you believe TSA should incorporate third-party auditing into future cybersecurity requirements and why, if you could?

Ms. SPAULDING. I do, Congressman. As you point out, we have numerous other places throughout the Government where third parties help to scale an effort that is put in place by the Government. My colleague here today, Patricia Cogswell, has made that comparison to the third party—the role of third parties in canine certification, for example.

So there is precedent for this, and I think it is an important way to scale. Our industry witnesses have talked about the need for speed in some of these certifications and for the Government to do the things it needs to do, and we know that CISA's resources are stretched.

Mr. LANGEVIN. Thank you very much.

I see my time has expired, so I am not going to add to my other two questions. But maybe I can submit them for the record, one on exploiting TSA regulations in other—to other sectors. The other one was on Government-sponsored testing of critical technologies. So I will submit those for the record, Madam Chair. Thank you. I yield back.

Thank you for your answers too, Suzanne, and to all our witnesses too. Thank you.

Madam Chair, you are on mute.

Mrs. WATSON COLEMAN. Thank you, Mr. Langevin. Thank you very much.

I want to thank the witnesses, not only for your very important expert testimony, but your forbearance during our delay. Thank you. We appreciate it.

Thank the Members for all of their questions today.

The Members of the subcommittees may have additional questions—as Mr. Langevin has noted he will—for you, and we ask that you respond expeditiously in writing to those questions. The Chair reminds the Members of the subcommittees that the committee's records will remain open for 10 days.

And so, with that, without objection, the subcommittees stand adjourned. Good day.

[Whereupon, at 5:01 p.m., the subcommittees were adjourned.]

Index

A

airports, 6, 18, 43, 55, 57, 87, 89, 95, 97, 121, 123, 124, 125, 148, 154
attacks, 2, 3, 4, 5, 8, 10, 19, 21, 37, 38, 39, 43, 44, 45, 46, 48, 55, 57, 59, 61, 62, 63, 71, 101, 102, 103, 104, 105, 121, 122, 124, 131, 136, 144, 160
auto industry, 90, 92

B

Biden, President, 5, 46, 66
breaches, vii, 2, 39, 61, 102, 104

C

Colonial Pipeline, 1, 2, 3, 4, 5, 6, 7, 9, 10, 23, 24, 27, 29, 31, 32, 34, 38, 39, 42, 43, 44, 46, 47, 55, 56, 57, 58, 61, 64, 67, 68, 70, 73, 79, 81, 82, 86, 88, 90, 92, 94, 96, 97, 98, 99, 101, 110, 114, 122, 124, 140, 157, 158, 159, 160
criminal organizations, 2, 38, 39
critical infrastructure, vii, 1, 3, 5, 8, 14, 16, 23, 29, 37, 39, 42, 45, 46, 47, 48, 55, 57, 60, 62, 63, 65, 66, 69, 70, 71, 72, 73, 75, 76, 77, 79, 82, 83, 86, 87, 88, 89, 91, 93, 94, 96, 97, 98, 100, 101, 102, 103, 104, 105, 106, 108, 109, 112, 114, 115, 116, 117, 118, 119, 120, 122, 124, 125, 127, 129, 130, 131, 133, 134, 135, 136, 137, 138, 139, 140, 143, 151, 157
cyberattack(s), vii, 1, 2, 4, 5, 8, 11, 14, 18, 19, 22, 23, 25, 28, 29, 36, 37, 38, 47, 55, 57, 58, 60, 62, 63, 64, 67, 70, 73, 77, 79, 87, 89, 90, 92, 94, 95, 97, 99, 100, 103, 104, 105, 114, 115, 118, 121, 122, 123, 124, 125, 127, 128, 131, 135, 139, 140, 148, 149, 151
cybersecurity, 1, 2, 3, 4, 5, 8, 13, 14, 15, 18, 19, 21, 22, 23, 27, 28, 29, 31, 32, 36, 38, 39, 45, 46, 47, 55, 56, 57, 58, 61, 62, 63, 64, 65, 66, 67, 68, 69, 70, 71, 73, 74, 75, 76, 77, 78, 79, 80, 81, 82, 83, 85, 86, 87, 88, 89, 90, 91, 92, 93, 94, 95, 96, 97, 98, 99, 100, 101, 102, 103, 104, 105, 106, 107, 108, 110, 111, 112, 115, 116, 117, 118, 119, 120, 122, 123, 125, 126, 127, 128, 129, 130, 131, 132, 133, 134, 135, 136, 137, 138, 139, 140, 141, 142, 143, 144, 145, 147, 148, 151, 154, 155, 156, 157, 158,159, 160
Cybersecurity and Infrastructure Security Agency (CISA), 2, 4, 5, 8, 9, 10, 14, 16, 17, 19, 27, 29, 30, 36, 39, 45, 56, 63, 64, 65, 66, 67, 69, 70, 71, 73, 76, 80, 86, 88, 90, 91, 92, 93, 99, 100, 101, 106, 107, 108, 111, 112, 113, 114, 116, 118, 119, 122, 125, 127, 128, 130, 131, 134, 135,

Index

136, 137, 138, 139, 140, 141, 142, 143, 144, 145, 146, 152, 160
cybersecurity incident, 1, 38, 56, 70, 86, 88, 106

D

DarkSide, 4, 5, 7, 12, 17, 27, 43, 48, 61
decryption key, 4
Department of Energy (DOE), 9, 16, 27, 29, 36, 45, 56, 66, 67, 69, 74, 80, 81, 132, 137
Department of Homeland Security (DHS), 2, 4, 5, 14, 35, 39, 45, 56, 60, 61, 63, 64, 65, 69, 71, 72, 74, 76, 77, 80, 86, 89, 90, 92, 100, 102, 104, 107, 108, 109, 110, 111, 113, 114, 115, 116, 117, 118, 119, 120, 122, 124, 125, 143, 145, 146, 147, 157, 158, 159
domestic cybersecurity, 8, 105

E

energy infrastructure, 6

F

Federal Bureau of Investigation (FBI), 2, 4, 5, 7, 8, 9, 10, 11, 12, 17, 20, 21, 22, 28, 29, 35, 36, 38, 44, 63, 101, 107, 121, 135, 142
Federal Energy Regulatory Commission (FERC), 9, 16, 45, 56, 61, 62, 69, 80, 81, 83
federal government, vii, 2, 5, 8, 10, 19, 32, 35, 37, 39, 45, 47, 58, 77, 81, 82, 86, 88, 89, 90, 92, 102, 104, 108, 112, 129, 130, 132, 133, 134, 135, 136, 137, 138, 139, 140, 143, 157, 158, 159
foreign adversaries, vii, 2, 37, 39
foreign governments, 2, 5, 15, 19, 38

G

gas shortages, 2, 38, 90, 92

H

hackers, 3, 4, 11, 13, 21, 89, 94, 95, 96, 106, 144
Homeland Security and Governmental Affairs Committee (HSGAC), 5

I

individual risk, vii, 2, 39
Industrial Control Systems (ICS), 58, 59, 60, 63, 66, 70, 74, 112, 115, 116, 118, 119, 120, 141, 142, 143
information technology (IT), 3, 4, 5, 7, 8, 9, 10, 11, 12, 13, 14, 15, 16, 17, 18, 19, 20, 21, 22, 23, 24, 25, 26, 27, 28, 29, 30, 31, 32, 33, 35, 36, 37, 39, 42, 43, 44, 45, 46, 47, 48, 55, 56, 58, 61, 62, 63, 64, 69, 71, 76, 77, 78, 80, 81, 87, 89, 91, 93, 94, 95, 97, 98, 99, 100, 101, 102, 103, 104, 106, 108, 109, 111, 112, 113, 114, 115, 117, 119, 120, 122, 125, 126, 127, 128, 129, 130, 131, 132, 134, 137, 138, 139, 141, 142, 143, 144, 145, 146, 147, 148, 149, 150, 151, 152, 153, 154, 155, 156, 157, 158, 159, 160, 161
infrastructure, vii, 2, 3, 5, 14, 16, 23, 24, 34, 37, 39, 42, 45, 47, 60, 61, 62, 63, 65, 66, 68, 69, 71, 73, 77, 81, 85, 86, 87, 90, 91, 93, 100, 102, 105, 108, 112, 115, 116, 118, 119, 129, 131, 136, 139, 141, 142, 146, 151, 152, 153, 158
Internet of Things (IoT), 58
Internet platforms, 2
internet protocol (IP) addresses, 10

Index

M

malicious software (malware), 44, 45, 60, 61, 62, 114, 152
Mandiant, 8, 9, 11, 13, 21, 22, 26, 27, 35, 36, 37, 44, 47
mass transit, 87, 89, 98, 150, 159
mass transit system, 87, 89, 150, 159
meat processor, 3
Metropolitan Transit Authority (MTA), 87, 89, 91, 93, 94, 96
multifactor authentication (MAF), 4, 13, 86

N

national security, 5, 22, 23, 37, 42, 45, 66, 74, 86, 89, 107, 115, 117, 118, 159
networks, vii, 2, 3, 8, 38, 39, 48, 59, 63, 64, 102, 106, 107, 141, 154

O

Obama, President, 86, 88
Office of Foreign Assets Control (OFAC), 12
operational technology (OT), 26, 27, 33, 44, 45, 46, 47, 55, 58, 59, 61, 64, 69, 71, 109, 113, 114, 141, 151

P

Pipeline and Hazardous Materials Safety Administration (PHMSA), 9, 16, 25, 45, 56, 57, 63, 71, 72, 73, 76, 80, 81, 112
pipeline cybersecurity, 55, 56, 57, 58, 61, 62, 64, 66, 67, 68, 69, 70, 71, 73, 75, 77, 80, 81, 82, 83, 113, 157
Pipeline Security Act, 55, 58, 67, 75, 81
pipeline system, 6, 11, 16, 33, 42, 43, 57, 60, 61, 62, 64, 66, 68, 69, 73, 74, 75

Promoting Interagency Coordination for Review of Natural Gas Pipelines Act, 55, 58, 81
Putin, President, 5

R

ransom(s), 2, 3, 4, 5, 7, 10, 12, 13, 18, 20, 21, 22, 28, 38, 43, 46, 61, 104, 105, 121, 124
ransomware, 2, 3, 4, 5, 7, 8, 10, 11, 20, 21, 22, 24, 25, 26, 29, 38, 39, 43, 47, 48, 55, 56, 57, 58, 61, 64, 68, 71, 73, 81, 82, 86, 88, 90, 92, 95, 97, 98, 99, 104, 105, 106, 110, 116, 119, 121, 122, 124, 125, 128, 141, 158, 159
ransomware hackers, 4
ransomware victims, 4, 61
remote access, 13
RSA token allowance, 13

S

sanctioned entity, 12
sanctioned individuals, 12
Sector Coordinating Council (SCC), 8, 69, 147
security screens, 9
sensitive victim data, 3
single-factor authentication, 13
SolarWinds hack, 2, 38
supervisory control and data acquisition (SCADA), 58, 59, 60, 62, 63, 69, 73, 74

T

terrorist groups, 61
transportation, 2, 14, 16, 30, 31, 38, 56, 59, 62, 63, 64, 65, 66, 67, 68, 70, 71, 72, 73, 77, 78, 79, 81, 83, 85, 86, 87, 88, 89, 90, 91, 92, 93, 94, 95, 96, 97, 98, 99, 100, 101, 107, 110, 112, 115, 116, 117, 118, 119, 120, 125, 129,

131, 132, 144, 145, 146, 150, 151,
  155, 157, 158, 159
Transportation Security Administration
  (TSA), 14, 16, 28, 31, 56, 62, 64, 65,
  66, 67, 68, 69, 70, 71, 72, 73, 74, 75,
  76, 77, 78, 79, 80, 81, 86, 87, 88, 89,
  90, 91, 92, 93, 94, 95, 96, 97, 98, 99,
  100, 101, 107, 108, 109, 110, 112,
  113, 114, 115, 116, 117, 118, 119,
  120, 122, 125, 129, 132, 135, 140,
  141, 142, 143, 144, 145, 154, 155,
  157, 159, 160, 161

V

victims, 2, 7, 8, 9, 20, 39, 43, 48, 61,
  101, 105, 106, 121, 124, 127
virtual private network (VPN), 4, 7, 13,
  23, 31, 35, 47, 86, 88